Getting the Most

BANG

for the

Education Buck

GETTING THE MOST

BANG

FOR THE

EDUCATION BUCK

Frederick M. Hess
Brandon L. Wright

EDITORS

TEACHERS COLLEGE PRESS

TEACHERS COLLEGE | COLUMBIA UNIVERSITY

NEW YORK AND LONDON

Published by Teachers College Press,® 1234 Amsterdam Avenue, New York, NY 10027

Library of Congress Cataloging-in-Publication Data

Names: Hess, Frederick M., editor. | Wright, Brandon L., editor.
Title: Getting the most bang for the education buck / edited by Frederick M. Hess, Brandon L. Wright.
Description: New York : Teachers College Press, 2020. | Includes bibliographical references and index.
Identifiers: LCCN 2020017705 (print) | LCCN 2020017706 (ebook) | ISBN 9780807764404 (paperback) | ISBN 9780807764411 (hardcover) | ISBN 9780807779101 (ebook)
Subjects: LCSH: Public schools—United States—Finance. | Public schools—United States—Cost effectiveness. | School budgets—United States.
Classification: LCC LB2825 .G45 2020 (print) | LCC LB2825 (ebook) | DDC 379.1/1—dc23
LC record available at https://lccn.loc.gov/2020017705
LC ebook record available at https://lccn.loc.gov/2020017706

ISBN 978-0-8077-6440-4 (paper)
ISBN 978-0-8077-6441-1 (hardcover)
ISBN 978-0-8077-7910-1 (ebook)

Printed on acid-free paper
Manufactured in the United States of America

Contents

PART III: GETTING STARTED

Acknowledgments

In recent years, up until March 2020, discussions of money in education had focused on calls to raise teacher pay, boost school spending, increase investments in infrastructure, and reallocate funds in ways deemed more "equitable." Whatever one's stance on any of these particular efforts, each of these conversations featured an implicit (oft-unspoken) presumption that the dollars in question would be spent wisely and well. Well, it's no great secret to observe that that's true sometimes, but not always. This book was rooted in the conviction that this implicit assumption needed to be much more explicit.

And then, while this book was well along, the coronavirus pandemic swept across the nation. It shuttered schools, devastated the economy, and torpedoed budgets. Suddenly, states and districts were intently focused on addressing the logistical and fiscal challenges. That made the contributions in this book that much more timely and relevant to educators, policymakers, and parents. The need to rethink how schools operate in a time of tight budgets is a daunting challenge, but may also provide opportunities to tackle changes that might have been regarded as too disruptive in more placid times.

The timeliness of this project is a reminder of another troubled time, the aftermath of the Great Recession of 2008 and 2009, which one of us tackled in an earlier volume titled *Stretching the School Dollar*. At that time, economic devastation and collapsing budgets meant that policymakers and educators were forced to ask: How might schools and districts save money while best serving kids? Events have conspired to make that question once again inescapable across the land. As it was back then, the challenge is not just to "save money" but to use the dollars we have more effectively—in ways that do more for students.

In an effort to elevate this question into the general discourse, we commissioned 12 scholars and analysts to offer their take on what we've learned in the past decade and to give specific suggestions for ways that schools and systems might get more bang for their buck. In October 2019, we hosted a research conference at the American Enterprise Institute (AEI) in Washington, DC, to hash this out. The volume you hold in your hands is the fruit of those efforts.

We are much obliged to all of those who have been involved in this project and have shaped our thinking. In particular, we would like to thank the authors, both for their conference drafts presented at the October 2019 conference and for the final chapters that appear here. In addition, we are deeply appreciative to the following discussants and panelists for their insights and feedback at the conference: Jim Blew, Joanne Weiss, Gerard Robinson, Daarel Burnette, and Amber M. Northern.

We are deeply indebted to AEI and its president, Robert Doar, as well as to the Thomas B. Fordham Institute and its president, Michael J. Petrilli, for their steadfast support. In addition, we are thankful that the Searle Freedom Trust, the Anschutz Family Foundation, the Thomas B. Fordham Institute, and AEI were able and willing to provide the resources and financial support required for this project. We'd like to offer special thanks to Chester E. Finn Jr., for his vital assistance in the editing of this volume. We'd also like to acknowledge the terrific staff at AEI, especially Hannah Warren for her work managing and overseeing this project, and her colleagues Brendan Bell, Sophia Martinson, Jessica Schurz, Olivia Shaw, Cade Grady, and Nathan May for their vital assistance. Finally, we once again want to express our gratitude to the wonderful Teachers College Press team, particularly executive acquisitions editor Brian Ellerbeck, who offered skillful and timely guidance throughout the course of this project.

Introduction

Brandon L. Wright

We set out working on this book guided by the conviction that we spend too much time talking about how much we should spend on schooling and not enough on how those dollars are spent. That seemed to us indisputably true, even as the national conversation tended to gravitate to assertions that we needed to spend more on schools, on teacher pay, or on a given program.

And then, while this book was well along, the United States was hit with COVID-19, and the immediacy of the challenge grew exponentially. Suddenly, schools faced unprecedented logistical challenges even as massive budget shortfalls loomed. All at once, schools were forced to rely on distance learning, provide devices and Internet access, and confront extraordinary uncertainty and public health challenges. The question of how to spend school dollars so that they do the most good for students took on a newfound urgency. The issues of technology, redesign, pensions, special education, and all the rest that the contributors explore are squarely on the agenda of every state and school system. Our hope is that this volume can serve as a resource and a guide for educators and policymakers as they navigate the challenges and seek the most bang for their education buck.

The school shutdowns and economic dislocations caused by COVID-19 unfolded against a backdrop of broad public support for school spending. In recent years, the "Red for Ed" movement has struck a particular chord, with teacher strikes in West Virginia, Oklahoma, Arizona, Los Angeles, Denver, and elsewhere putting a spotlight on whether states and districts can afford to pay what it takes to attract and retain terrific educators. Schools are seeking ways to offer advanced coursework to more students, and to expand their efforts in career and technical education, early childhood education, and social and emotional learning. Meanwhile, K–12 spending is squeezed by health care and pension obligations, the policy preferences of a graying population, and now COVID-19's hit to government revenue.

Educational leaders are understandably loath to cut current outlays to finance new priorities, but few communities are wholly satisfied with the status quo. And an emerging body of research finds a predictable, positive relationship between more funding and better student outcomes. That's why the focus of most leaders remains on raising new funds, raising teacher salaries, and promoting more "equitable" funding systems.

Yet whether or not the push for new funds is successful, educational leaders must decide how to spend those dollars in ways that make a difference. Indeed, one of the more bizarre education debates of the past quarter century has been over "does money matter?" It's tough to think of anywhere else in American life where we'd even have that discussion. Of course money matters. But a remarkable amount of attention has been devoted to the notion that it doesn't, as well as the equally dubious idea that more money is the answer to all of our educational ills.

While this familiar debate has gotten a lot of mileage, it tends to not represent the stance of serious disputants on either side of the issue. Few school spending skeptics argue that money can't help; they fear that funds will be spent on things that they deem unlikely to make a difference for students. And those who champion more spending typically concede that of course it matters how those funds are spent. In other words, nearly everyone agrees that spending is never just about "how much," but also a matter of "how."

Meanwhile, there can be a surprising lack of attention devoted to strategies for spending funds wisely and effectively. Indeed, accounts of "high-performing" schools and systems tend to focus intently on questions of instruction, assessment, leadership, and governance—not on spending strategies. That's likely why books like *Stretching the School Dollar*, the 2010 volume edited by Rick Hess, were well received—educators, school and system leaders, policymakers, funders, and advocates were hungry for practical thoughts about how to make dollars go further. That is the timely question that contributors tackle in this volume.

TODAY'S SCHOOL SPENDING ENVIRONMENT

The focus of this book is not on "cutting costs" but on identifying insights, lessons, and suggestions that can help schools spend their funds effectively.

This tack has particular resonance in today's context, which has seen states and communities fare very differently in the aftermath of the 2008–2009 Great Recession. More than a decade later, for example, there is less funding for education in a dozen states, after adjusting for inflation, than before the downturn. In some places, the gap is substantial—reaching 20% in Texas and nearly that much in Oklahoma and Alabama. At the same time, spending generally has trended upward in recent years, to levels making up about three-quarters of the ground lost. In such an environment, what education leaders and policymakers repeatedly tell us they want is practical guidance on how to make each dollar go further—whether a given dollar is "old" or "new."

Such advice is especially useful at a time when the prospects for more funding are uncertain. One reason is the public's mixed take on school spending. As we noted above, when the public is asked simply whether schools need more money, the answer is unequivocally *yes*. However, when folks are asked the same question after being told how much is already being spent on each student, public opinion divides—with Republicans, in particular, becoming much more skeptical of increased spending. When respondents are told that 90% of K–12 funding comes from state and local taxes, and not the federal government, nearly two-thirds oppose local increases.[1]

A second reason for caution is that while a growing body of research (discussed at greater length in Chapter 3) suggests the unsurprising observation that more school spending seems generally to lead to improved educational outcomes, there's an important and equally unsurprising caveat: How those dollars are spent, and how those plans are executed, matter immensely. And indeed, there are big concerns with the spate of calls to simply shower more money on schools. For one, there's a lack of assurance that funds will be spent wisely or well. The United States already spends about $700 billion on K–12 public education a year, or nearly $14,000 per student. That puts the United States pretty near the head of the pack internationally, even though our outcomes are far more disappointing. More money certainly could help, but even big increases can pale alongside those numbers, while leaving questions about why the new dollars will have a bigger impact than the old ones. It's vital that new spending be married to sensible changes and a commitment to spend existing funds more intelligently.

The third reason for leaders to be cautious about being bailed out by more funding is that existing policies and practices mean that a significant portion of any new spending would not flow to teachers, instructional materials, and students—but rather to obligations that have little to do with what happens in classrooms. Of particular import are skyrocketing health care and pension costs, especially for retirees (all of which is discussed at length in Chapter 2). The cost of health care has far outpaced inflation for decades, and although this has affected most American workers, governments have been particularly slow to adjust, which has had a significant effect on public-sector employees like teachers, two-thirds of whom work in states or districts that offer health benefits to retirees. Nationwide, just 7% of the projected future health care costs for public-sector retirees is covered. And 15 states, including populous ones like New York and Florida, have set aside zero dollars. On the pension front, almost every state has over-promised and under-saved. The states have now amassed a combined $500 billion in unfunded pension debt due to current and future public-sector retirees. It's grown so large and burdensome that just 30 cents of every dollar spent on pension promises goes toward today's workers.[2]

Dealing with accrued debts and obligations would be difficult for school systems in any environment, but it promises to be especially daunting during a time when America's population is graying. As explained at length in Chapter 1, this represents a big and growing challenge for schools. People over the age of 65 are less likely to support additional money for schools, preferring instead that it go to targets like health care or police programs. And the proportion of the population in that group is growing as the baby boomer generation, comprising those born between 1946 and 1964, ages. Their population exceeds 75 million people, making it the biggest adult group in the country. Moreover, a large majority are already older than the average retirement age for teachers—which, at 59, is younger than for most other professionals. In just 3 years' time, every single baby boomer will be past 59. This means that the current and growing strain on government coffers caused by obligations to retirees and other elderly residents is already significant and will persist for years to come. A graying population also matters because retirees tend to live on fixed incomes, so they tend to pay less in taxes, and an aging population correlates with lower rates of economic growth. The likely effect is that an aging population will decrease public support for additional school spending, increase the retiree costs of states and school systems, lessen the tax revenue available to fund those costs, make it more difficult to raise tax rates to cover the difference, and potentially contribute to a slower rate of economic growth.

This list of challenges is, of course, non-exhaustive. Other forces loom large for state policymakers and education leaders. These include special education obligations, teacher strikes and other union actions, shifting political trends, the rise and fall of various reforms, and, of course, the blow to public revenues caused by the COVID-19 pandemic. In the end, the situation is clear: School systems and their students could use more funding, but securing as much money as educators and advocates would like will be a tall order.

HOPE AND OPPORTUNITY

But all is not doom and gloom. Instead, this is a great opportunity for education leaders to make smarter decisions with their money. No one makes tough choices in flush times. No executive in the public or the private sector is eager to squeeze salaries, shut down inefficient programs, or trim employees when it can be avoided. This is why tough times can be so healthful for organizations. They make occasional pruning possible. They prod managers to tackle problems that otherwise get swept under the rug. This permits organizations to regain their fighting trim, reexamine old priorities, and create a leaner culture focused on productivity and performance.

In the aftermath of the Great Recession, for example, this is exactly what happened. Financially strapped, many districts found ways to do more with whatever they had. To avoid layoffs, New York City instituted a cost-of-living wage freeze. Others asked employees to make concessions on their salaries or benefits by doing things like contributing more to their health insurance plans.

Although we didn't expect to find ourselves in such a dire financial situation so soon, the COVID-19 pandemic gives courageous leaders new cause to make—and new rationales to justify—smart, necessary decisions about how to spend school funds. That's where this volume comes in. Whether or not school leaders get all the resources they might need or desire, they can make the dollars they do have go further by finding ways to get more bang for the education buck.

In the chapters ahead, contributors will explore a panoply of such possibilities. They will discuss how districts and schools can rethink staffing and management to get more value for employee compensation; how policymakers might revisit pension arrangements so as to control costs while putting more money in teachers' pockets; how educators can more powerfully leverage technology; and how districts might assess options differently in order to more fully address the needs of students.

THE BOOK FROM HERE

The book is split into three Parts. Part I explains how we got to this point, where school systems across the country are already struggling with a bevy of financial challenges that stand to get worse in coming years. Parts II and III are focused on solutions—ways school systems can prioritize and make trade-offs that can help them spend their dollars more effectively—with the former focused on more general lessons for how leaders can and should think about these issues, and the latter offering policy-specific recommendations.

In Chapter 1, Matthew Ladner, executive editor of redefinED, a choice-based education organization, will explain what a graying population means for school spending—a topic he's focused on during his long career in education policy. For some time now, and daily until 2030, an average of 10,000 baby boomers per day reach the age of 65 in America. This impacts state budgets and K–12 education in major ways—from less public support for funding increases, to straining debts and obligations for retiree benefits, to reducing tax revenue and even accelerating our path to a new recession. This chapter sets up many of the reasons why this book is timely and important today.

In Chapter 2, Chad Aldeman, senior associate partner at Bellwether Education Partners and a leading expert on the pension and health care problems facing schools, will explain those issues and how to address them. Over the past 2 decades, teacher salaries have not kept up with inflation, even as teachers' total compensation packages have. And the primary cause is the accelerating costs of health care and retirement benefits. These costs are straining school district budgets and limiting teacher salary growth, but remain largely hidden from most teachers and the general public. This chapter describes how we got into this situation, discusses what it means for leaders worried about funding levels, explains why the current systems are not working well for teachers or schools, and explores potential options for reform.

Chapter 3 examines the relationship between school funding and student outcomes. It's written by Adam Tyner, associate director of research at the Thomas B. Fordham Institute, who previously has designed custom research projects focused on school finance while working with district administrators in many of the nation's large school systems. A burgeoning collection of research has positively linked higher levels of school funding to improved student outcomes, especially for disadvantaged students. This chapter synthesizes these predictable results, but also demonstrates why *what* that money is spent on matters immensely. The takeaway is that regardless of whether stakeholders are able to increase funding, they should always focus on spending wisely whatever money they have.

In Chapter 4, which kicks off Part II of the volume, Michael Q. McShane, director of national research at EdChoice, profiles schools and systems that have successfully done what this volume is meant to facilitate—gotten more bang for their buck. Ask almost any school board member or superintendent and they'll tell you that they're already "stretching the school dollar." But while such decisions sometimes may make good sense, they are rarely the stuff of transformative improvement. There are, however, exceptions, and this chapter looks at three that took the idea of finding efficiencies seriously: one public school district, one charter school, and one private school. These organizations did not make marginal changes. They worked to fundamentally rethink how they delivered education to their students.

Chapter 5 is written by Marguerite Roza, director of the Edunomics Lab at Georgetown University, and an expert who has written extensively about school finance. Here she explores a thought experiment: What if you computed the per-student cost of educational services—like pre-K, class-size reductions, transportation, or special education services—and then asked families, "Would you rather have the service or a cost-neutral alternative?" Asking the question can help us think differently about routine decisions. The exercise isn't a policy proposal per se; rather, it's a tool for gauging what services really cost, so that their value can be appropriately weighed. Where families would prefer the cash, it's a signal that value may be lacking or that spending should be aggressively scrutinized.

In Chapter 6, Bryan Hassel and Emily Ayscue Hassel, co-presidents of Public Impact, an education policy organization that focuses in part on education funding, suggest ways systems can rethink school staffing to make their dollars go further. Most U.S. educational spending goes toward salaries and benefits—not just of teachers, but of the half of all staff who are not directly responsible for student learning. Districts overwhelmingly use the same basic "one-teacher, one-classroom" staffing model for their schools, with all teachers reporting to the principal. Over the past 40 years, schools have added a panoply of other personnel to support this model, reduced class sizes and added more teachers, and kept teacher pay per hour largely flat, when adjusted for inflation. This isn't sustainable. But fortunately, there are better ways to handle school staffing, and this chapter explores them.

Part III of the volume kicks off with Chapter 7, written by Scott Milam, Carrie Stewart, and Katie Morrison-Reed, all of whom work at Afton Partners, a consulting firm that has collaborated with over 100 schools in developing long-term financial plans centered around technology-based models. In other sectors, tech has lowered costs and boosted productivity, but that isn't generally true yet in K–12 education. That represents an opportunity, and this chapter explains how leaders can take advantage of it, focusing on several districts that have already done so successfully, as well as some that have failed, and why.

In Chapter 8, Karen Hawley Miles, chief executive officer and president of Education Resource Strategies, explains ways in which the many districts across the country facing declining enrollment can better deal with the problem. At first blush, the idea of "stretching" the school dollar in the context of declining enrollment seems like an oxymoron. But declining enrollment creates constant budget pressure that too often squeezes out innovation and investment. Drawing on specific examples from districts like Denver and Baltimore, this chapter explores what districts can do to get out of this squeeze and tackle challenges in more constructive ways.

Chapter 9, the last in the volume, is authored by Nathan Levenson, managing director of the District Management Group and author of multiple books on school finance. Here he discusses a more effective and more cost-efficient approach to special education—which in its present form is comprised of high costs, low levels of learning, frustrated parents, and staff who are leaving the profession in droves. The culprit is 20 years of reforms centered around the idea that more is better—more minutes, more teachers, more spending. This chapter offers a better approach based on three shifts in thinking and practice: more general education, rather than more special education; more time to learn, not less content to learn; and more highly skilled adults, not more adults. Districts that have embraced this approach have raised achievement dramatically even as costs were reduced or kept steady.

IT'S WHAT SCHOOLS DO WITH MONEY THAT MATTERS

There is plenty of research and writing on education finance, but much of it is focused on questions of adequacy and equity in raising and allocating education funds. That valuable work can be understood as examining the "revenue" side of the educational ledger. There is, however, a dearth of guidance about the other side of the ledger—how dollars are spent and, more important, how they can be spent more effectively.

Where's the help for schools and systems that want to spend the money they have—or the money they'll get—more effectively? There's long been a lack of such advice, and its causes are unclear. When Rick Hess's 2010 edited volume *Stretching the School Dollar* was published, he and I were struck by the same problem. "Perhaps it's because education spending historically has risen year after year," we pondered. "Perhaps it's because educators and reformers prefer to focus on boosting achievement rather than cost-effectiveness. Perhaps it's because the data systems to track and monitor cost-effectiveness traditionally have not been available. Perhaps it's a question of educational culture."

Ultimately, whatever the cause, we hope this volume will prove to be a useful resource for practitioners and policymakers alike. With that, let's get started.

NOTES

1. Figures come from the 2019 EdNext Poll. See https://www.educationnext .org/2019-ednext-poll-interactive

2. See, for example, www.theatlantic.com/education/archive/2016/05/what -teachers-lose-to-pension-debt/482673

Part I

WHERE WE ARE

CHAPTER 1

American Schools Look to a Challenging Funding Future

Matthew Ladner

The past 11 years saw the national debt nearly double as a share of GDP, bringing it to a level not seen since shortly after World War II. If policy changes are not so abrupt as to hinder economic growth, then the sooner policies are adopted to avert these trends, the smaller the changes to revenue and/or spending that would be required to achieve sustainability over the long term. While the estimated magnitude of the fiscal gap is subject to a substantial amount of uncertainty, there is little doubt that current policy is not sustainable.

—U.S. Treasury, *Financial Report of the United States Government,* Fiscal Year 2018

If something cannot go on forever, it will stop.

—Herbert Stein

In February 2008, the oldest known American baby boomer—a retired teacher named Kathleen Casey-Kirschling—received the first Social Security check of her generation. Born 1 minute after midnight in 1946, Casey-Kirschling took early retirement at age 62. By 2011, the oldest baby boomers had reached 65, and by 2014, the youngest boomers had reached 50. Half of this massive generation will have reached 65 by 2021. Nine years later, *all* surviving members will have attained that milestone, the traditional age of retirement for working Americans. By 2035, the Census Bureau projects, the elderly will outnumber the young for the first time in U.S. history (Vespa et al., 2018). The implications are profound for every public service and governmental function in the land, including K–12 education.

The baby boom generation started after World War II in 1946 and ended in 1964, during which approximately 76,000,000 Americans were born. It reached its peak earning years during the 1980s and 1990s—which helped to finance increased spending on both K–12 education for their children and health care for their parents.

Federal entitlement programs—Social Security and Medicare—primarily come to mind when the topic of aging baby boomers is raised, and for good reason. Reports from both programs show massive unfunded liabilities and depleting trust funds.

K–12 education, however, is financed primarily by states and localities, with federal funds typically constituting 8–10% of school operating budgets. But the risk to K–12 funding from massive demographic changes is far greater than that, for the federal government provides over 30% of the average state's total budget. An Uncle Sam struggling to keep entitlement programs functional may leave states facing some difficult decisions.

Moreover, an aging population has direct impacts on state finances. People in their peak earning years pay a lot of taxes, but retirees live on fixed incomes. Larger elderly populations correlate with slower rates of economic growth, and thus with slower state revenue growth. Larger numbers of elderly residents lead to increased spending on Medicaid and other services. And that's without even considering a huge fiscal challenge that states already face, arising from lawmakers' generous contributions to state employees' pensions during the late 1990s "dot com" stock market boom, when many systems had more money than needed to pay future beneficiaries. Today, state pension systems face large structural deficits despite large increases in required contributions from current employees, including teachers and the school systems for which they work.

Sometimes termed "the Gray Tsunami" or "Hurricane Gray," the retirement of the baby-boom generation will represent an unprecedented challenge to American public services of every sort (Taylor & Pew Research Center, 2014, p. 17; see also Wheelwright, 2012). Our public schools enjoyed decades of nearly uninterrupted funding increases—typically gauged in inflation-adjusted, per-pupil dollars—throughout the 20th century and into the 21st. The growing ability and willingness of American policymakers and taxpayers to boost per-pupil funding signaled both the broad economic success of American society during that period and its willingness to invest in its children's future. Despite enormous controversies surrounding the equity and effectiveness of our K–12 spending, the near-constant increase in per-pupil education dollars is impressive in both scope and consistency.

Circumstances, however, may be conspiring to bring a profound change to this trend. Indeed, we probably will look back upon the almost nonstop increases in American per-pupil funding between 1919 and the advent of the Great Recession in 2008 as a golden age of resources. MIT economist James M. Poterba has found that an increase in a jurisdiction's elderly population leads to a decrease in school spending per child. Many elderly people live on fixed incomes and thus may prefer to avoid tax increases (Poterba, 1996).

The main challenge ahead for school spending may prove to be increased demand for alternative spending priorities.

Public school spending is a function of our ability and willingness to direct money there. Polls show a broad misunderstanding of how much is spent on public education, as well as a broad desire to spend more (Henderson et al., & West, 2019). Thus our *desire* to spend more on K–12 may continue indefinitely, even as we have mounting reasons to doubt our *ability* to do that.

Public support for K–12 education is guaranteed in state constitutions, and opinion polls show that it's also written on the hearts of Americans. Despite the challenges ahead, it is in no danger of being abolished. But the worst-case scenario going forward looks challenging indeed. Our schools improved their performance only modestly during decades of sustained funding increases. As the demand for public health, pension, and entitlement spending rises, the worst-case scenario involves the education system retaining its shortcomings while losing a nontrivial amount of funding.

The best-case scenario, of course, is that American schools improve outcomes within a more austere financial environment. Other chapters of this volume suggest ways that may be possible. Here I explain further how we got to this point, and why doing more with less—that is, boosting the effectiveness and efficiency of our K–12 enterprise—is becoming more urgent.

THE TENSION BETWEEN HEALTH, PENSION, AND EDUCATION SPENDING IN STATE BUDGETS

Polling data by the Pew Center have established large differences on a variety of political and policy issues between the generations now living in the United States (Parker et al., 2019). Broadly speaking, the financial interests of the elderly lie in health care and pensions, while young adults have a competing demand for K–12 and university investments. During the latter half of the 20th century, Americans increased their investment in all these things, expanding entitlement benefits for the elderly while also increasing K–12 funding. The massive baby-boom generation reached its peak earning years during the 1980s and 1990s, providing considerable tax revenue, although also running up considerable debt. One can only marvel at what sustained economic growth and a confident government debt market can deliver.

During the peak earning years of the baby boomers, the United States effectively increased spending on everything. This was abetted by a long period of very favorable age demography: a relatively small generation of retirees, a large working-age generation, and a relatively small school-age generation. But spending increased at a greater rate for the areas that baby boomers cared about most.

Indeed, since the turn of the 21st century, the only expenditure category to increase as a percentage of all state spending in every state has been Medicaid. All other categories have declined or been flat as percentages of total state spending, according to the National Association of State Budget Officers. Specifically, across all 50 states, K–12 education declined from 23.9% of total state spending in 1988 to 19.6% in 2018, while Medicaid spending increased from 11.5% to 29.7%.

There are multiple reasons for these trends, the most obvious being that Medicaid is financed by a system of matching funds from the federal government to states. If Washington, DC, had chosen to match spending on other categories, it's likely that they too would have increased.

State dollars spent on Medicaid obviously cannot be spent on other priorities, including K–12 education. While federal Medicaid matching dollars may seem like "free money" to state budgetmakers, they are anything but to both taxpayers and other funding priorities within state government.

Despite public education being squeezed as a percentage of state budget spending between 1988 and 2018, inflation-adjusted, per-pupil spending continued to increase nationally. The tension between state health and education spending has been largely manageable over previous decades, as it has been possible for both types of spending to increase, albeit in different ways. Going forward, however, with an aging population, continued increases in health spending will put pressure on all other categories of state spending, including K–12 education. The favorable conditions that led to increased spending across the board during baby boomers' peak earning years will disappear as the baby boomers exit work and enter old-age entitlement programs.

Indeed, the elderly are among the heaviest users of the Medicaid program on a per-enrollee basis. The so-called "super-elderly" population, aged 85 and above, make especially large claims on Medicaid, due in large part to nursing home and hospice care. In 2011, Medicaid enrollees over the age of 85 drew upon Medicaid resources at more than twice the rate of those aged 65 to 74. The U.S. Census Bureau (2010) projects that those aged 85 and over will increase from 5.7 million in 2010 to 19.1 million by 2050 (p. 10).

In 1988, Congress required states participating in the Medicaid program to cover health costs not covered by Medicare for low-income residents and those possessing less than a specified level of financial assets (Rowland & Lyons, 1996). This action linked the two programs and created an additional state obligation for funding.

Simultaneously, these demographic changes also will restrict the supply of public dollars collected by states due to slower economic growth, and this will increase pension liabilities. The elderly typically have passed their prime earning years. States with growing elderly populations can expect to see a slower rate of tax revenue growth as the elderly earn and spend less. Several economists also expect the aging of the population to slow the national rate of economic growth.

Lower rates of economic growth naturally result in a slower rate of revenue growth for government. Northwestern University economist Robert J. Gordon forecasts a decelerating rate of economic growth for the American economy, down to an annual rate of 0.9% for the 2007–2047 period.

Anything close to such a low rate of growth would cause severe fiscal difficulties in state budgets, especially given today's whopping state and local pension issues. Collectively, state and local pension plans went from a $1.4 trillion funding shortfall in 2002 to a $4.2 trillion shortfall at the end of 2016 (Board of Governors of the Federal Reserve Bank, 2019).

ORGANIZATION AND FAVORABLE DEMOGRAPHICS ENABLE K–12 FUNDING INCREASES

Americans organized their publicly funded K–12 education arrangements into local government districts during the 1800s. The dominant model across almost all states settled on boards of elected officials governing school districts. School boards set local policies and hire a superintendent to run the district. Districts until recently held a monopoly on public schooling options within their geographic territory, and within districts each school had an attendance boundary in which it was the exclusive provider of public education. The advent of charter schools and other forms of school choice have weakened that monopoly status, but districts continue to educate 82% of students in their schools (some of which are schools of choice) at the time of this writing.

School district elections are often low-turnout affairs conducted with limited information available to voters, typically outside of the standard November election dates. This is related in part to collective bargaining and the unionization of educators, as well as other advocacy groups that have ample funding and influence. Together they exercise enormous influence in low-turnout, low-visibility board elections and play a very large role in determining K–12 education policy at the state and federal levels.

This has led to increased school spending and hiring. The average American public school student cost taxpayers $5,242 in 1969–1970, for example, but $12,533 in 2014–2015 in constant dollars (U.S. Department of Education, 2017).

Educational outcomes have not kept pace. American high school seniors score poorly on international exams of academic achievement, and the most reliable longitudinal data (the results of the National Assessment of Educational Progress) show largely flat scores since the early 1970s. With spending up and achievement flat, America has suffered a collapse in the return on its investment in K–12 education.

STATES WILL VARY IN THE SCALE OF THE CHALLENGE

Demographers calculate age dependency ratios, and economists have found that those ratios predict rates of economic growth. An age dependency ratio essentially compares the number of young and elderly people in a population to the number of working-age residents.

From the perspective of a state budgeting agency, young people don't work, don't pay taxes, and go to school. And as stated, older people are out of the prime earning years and often use Medicaid heavily. An age dependency ratio basically reveals the number of people in the young and old categories compared with the number of people in neither—that is, those of typical working age.

The United States had a youth-led increase in the age dependency ratio during the 1950s and 1960s as the baby-boom generation went through the K–12 system. By 1980, almost all boomers had aged out of school, and the nation's age dependency ratio stood at 65, declining further to 59 in 2010. This is to say, for every 100 working-age residents, the United States had 59 people in either the youth or elderly categories. But as boomers get older, the age dependency ratio will rise. It's projected to be 65 in 2020 and 75 or thereabouts in 2030 and beyond.

The impact will not be uniform across the country, however. All states will grow older in the coming years and decades, but proportions will vary, and some also will see increases in their youth population. Indeed, by 2030, New Mexico and South Dakota are expected to have age dependency ratios of more than 90, while Washington's is projected to be south of 70. In 2010, only one state had a ratio higher than that.

The growth in youth will be caused not only by births, but also by movement from other states and countries. And the Digest of Education Statistics projects the variance between states to be significant. Florida, North Dakota, and Washington, for example, are expected to see school-age growth rates north of 15% between 2015 and 2027, while the school-age populations in Connecticut and New Hampshire are expected to fall by more than 10%.

States with increasing populations face a near-certainty of cost increases in the absence of more efficient delivery of services, but states with declining enrollment have their own unique set of struggles, as Karen Hawley Miles explores in Chapter 8, and have not realized cost savings consistently. For example, between 2000 and 2018, 18 states experienced reductions in the size of their public K–12 populations, but only one of these states (Michigan) experienced a decline in per-pupil funding, and this was of a modest nature. Maine, New Hampshire, and Vermont each saw enrollments fall more than 10% during this period, but Maine's per-pupil funding increased by 30%, and New Hampshire's and Vermont's by more than 60% (Petrilli, 2019). The ability of states to realize cost savings can fail to materialize due to economies of scale issues and community opposition to school consolidation.

CONCLUSION: SURVIVING AND THRIVING IN A CHALLENGING FUTURE

The world is a much better place in many ways now than when Kathleen Casey-Kirschling, the first baby boomer, was born. Americans made significant progress in addressing voting and civil rights and put a man on the moon in the span of a single decade. We saw substantial declines in rates of global poverty. The baby-boom generation is exiting its working-age years having produced technological marvels, with more almost certainly on the way.

Yet boomers also are bequeathing to younger generations an unsustainable set of social welfare institutions. Meeting this challenge will be difficult and will cause hardships for other public institutions like schools, but it could be far worse. The mothers and fathers of boomers, for instance, inherited a worldwide economic depression that dominated their childhood. Just in time for their 20s, they found themselves obligated to fight and win a world war against global fascism. Following that, a tense standoff of nuclear brinkmanship against the Soviet Union lasted the entirety of their working lives.

Adapting the American social welfare state for a new set of circumstances constitutes an entirely modest challenge by comparison—but it's one that has eluded us thus far. Increasing the productivity of public spending on education and health, while balancing the revenues and expenditures of entitlement and pension programs, does indeed seem daunting. But we can't avoid it forever. And the fundamental changes in our society mean we ought to take on the challenge now.

The chapters ahead will provide suggestions on how states, districts, and school leaders can do this in practice. Let's get on with it.

REFERENCES

Board of Governors of the Federal Reserve Bank. (2019). *State and local government pension funding status, 2002–2017.* https://www.federalreserve.gov/releases/z1/dataviz/pension/funding_status/table

Henderson, M. B., Houston, D., Peterson P. E., & West, M. R. (2019). Public support grows for higher teacher pay and expanded school choice. *Education Next,* 20(1). https://www.educationnext.org/school-choice-trump-era-results-2019-education-next-poll

Parker, K., Graf, N., & Igielnik, R. (2019). *Generation Z looks a lot like millennials on key social and political issues.* Pew Research Center. https://www.pewsocialtrends.org/2019/01/17/generation-z-looks-a-lot-like-millennials-on-key-social-and-political-issues

Petrilli, M. (2019). The baby bust goes to school. *Education Next, 19*(3). www
   .educationnext.org/baby-bust-goes-to-school-falling-birthrates-crisis-opportunity

Poterba, J. (1996). *Demographic structure and the political economy of public education* (Working Paper No. 5677). National Bureau of Economic Research.
   www.nber.org/papers/w5677

Rowland, D., & Lyons, B. (1996). Medicare, Medicaid, and the elderly poor. *Health
   Care Financing Review, 18*(2), 65–66. www.ssa.gov/history/pdf/Rowlandand
   Lyons.pdf

Taylor, P., & Pew Research Center. (2014). *The next America: Boomers, millennials
   and the looming generational showdown.* Public Affairs.

U.S. Census Bureau. (2010, May). *The next four decades: The older population in
   the United States: 2010 to 2050.* www.census.gov/prod/2010pubs/p25-1138.pdf

U.S. Department of Education, National Center for Education Statistics. (2017, October). *Table 236.70: Current expenditure per pupil in average daily attendance
   in public elementary and secondary schools, by state or jurisdiction: Selected years, 1969–70 through 2014–15.* nces.ed.gov/programs/digest/d17/tables
   /dt17_236.70.asp

Vespa, J., Medina, L., & Armstrong, D. (2018). *Demographic turning points:
   Population projections for the United States: 2020 to 2060.* U.S. Census Bureau. www.census.gov/content/dam/Census/newsroom/press-kits/2018/jsm/jsm
   -presentation-pop-projections.pdf

Wheelwright, J. (2012, September 18). *The gray tsunami.* Discover Magazine.
   https://www.discovermagazine.com/health/the-gray-tsunami

CHAPTER 2

How to Address the Rising Cost of Employee Benefits

Chad Aldeman

INTRODUCTION

As a wave of teacher strikes hit the country throughout 2018 and 2019, teachers had a right to be mad. On average, their salaries had not kept up with inflation for the prior 2 decades, and teacher salaries were losing ground compared with those of other similarly educated professionals.

While that may be the part of the story that teachers saw, it ignores what their employers knew: Due to the rapidly rising costs of teacher benefits, the cost to employ any individual teacher had risen considerably.[1] In fact, once those benefit costs are included, it turns out that total teacher compensation has more than kept up with inflation over time, even as base salaries have not.

In other words, there's a growing disconnect between what teachers see in their paychecks and what their employers pay to employ them. This situation may be hidden from teachers, who may not be conscious of what's not there. But it does still affect them. After all, teachers can't buy groceries or pay their mortgage with their employer's pension or health care contributions.

This is not a one-time trend that will clear up on its own. For decades now, health care costs have escalated much faster than inflation, eating into the paychecks of nearly all American workers. This is an economy-wide phenomenon, although it is also true that public-sector employers, including school district leaders, have been particularly slow to respond. As noted in Chapter 1 and explored in more depth in Chapter 8, student enrollment growth has slowed or even declined in some areas. Assuming districts are able to keep their staffing ratios constant, changes in student enrollment should not drive higher health care costs per teacher.

The situation is more dire, however, in places where states have built up unfunded liabilities. For retiree health and pension benefits, states have over-promised and under-saved, leading to a significant fixed debt that must be paid, even if student enrollment declines.

On the retirement side, the cost increases are due entirely to the structures put in place by state legislatures. Every state created defined benefit (DB) pension plans that promised benefits according to formulas based on the worker's salary and years of service. To determine how much they needed to contribute to those benefits, states hired actuaries to make assumptions about things like how fast payroll would grow, how long teachers would stay, when they would retire, how long retirees would live (and collect benefits), and how fast investments would grow in the future. If any of these assumptions was wrong, or if states didn't make the contributions the actuaries thought were necessary, the pension plan would accumulate unfunded liabilities.[2]

Although there's been a slow but steady evolution away from DB pension plans in the private sector, they still cover 90% of public schoolteachers. Nearly every state has over-promised and under-saved for teacher retirement benefits, and collectively the plans covering teachers owe more than $500 billion in unfunded pension promises due to current and future retirees.[3] Those debts have risen over time and now loom as a large intergenerational wealth transfer from current and future teachers to pay off the debts owed to their predecessors. These Ponzi schemes are particularly apparent in states with declining enrollment, where the debt overhang acts like a fixed cost on a declining revenue base. In response, states have increased employer and employee contribution rates and cut benefits for new and future teachers.

This chapter will look at the financial challenges presented by the growing creep of benefit costs for public schoolteachers. It starts by outlining the big picture of how teacher pension and health care costs have changed over time. While it may not surprise readers that teachers receive more generous benefits than workers in other sectors, it may be surprising just how severely those costs have risen over time and how those macro trends have directly and indirectly affected regular classroom teachers in the here and now. The chapter then delves into particular issues around pension and health care benefits, including a discussion of the recruitment and retention effects of those benefits as compared with alternatives, such as paying teachers higher base salaries. Finally, it concludes with suggestions that state and district leaders could take to address their growing benefit obligations. States will need to make political trade-offs to reverse the long-term trends and start to put more money directly into teachers' pockets.

NATIONAL TRENDS IN TEACHER COMPENSATION

According to the U.S. Department of Education (2017), teacher salaries haven't increased, in inflation-adjusted terms, since the late 1980s. That is, even as education spending increased overall, each individual employee received a smaller and smaller share of the overall budget.[4]

One factor is the personnel employed in our schools and district central offices. Over time, districts have lowered both the teacher–student and administrator–student ratios.

But the structure of teacher compensation has also changed over time. While *base teacher salaries* have not increased, *total teacher compensation costs* have risen, driven by large increases in health care and retirement costs. Total per-pupil spending rose 36% over the past 2 decades, in constant dollars, whereas spending on salaries and wages rose just 21%. Meanwhile, spending on employee benefits increased 98%.

The education field is not alone in this trend. Across all sectors of the economy, benefit costs are rising faster than inflation, as the baby-boom generation ages and begins to retire. In real terms, civilian employer payments for health care and retirement costs rose 7% and 26%, respectively. For public school districts, however, insurance costs over the same time period rose by 10% in real terms, and retirement costs rose by 76% ("Employer Costs," 2020).

As a percentage of worker compensation, teacher health care costs are on the high end, but they are not an extreme outlier. In contrast, teachers have by far the highest retirement costs, even compared with other public-sector employees. While the average civilian employer pays $1.92 for retirement benefits per hour worked, and the average state and local government employer pays $6.00, public school districts are paying $8.87 per hour in retirement compensation. As a percentage of their total compensation package, teacher retirement benefits eat up more than twice as much as for other workers (13.3% vs. 5.4%).

Current and future teachers are not the primary beneficiaries of these expenditures. In fact, much of these costs are going toward paying down unfunded promises, not as benefit enhancements for teachers. These trends are unlikely to reverse anytime soon, and state leaders will need to think differently about the benefit packages they offer if they want to see any future improvements. The next sections provide more detail about each of these benefit categories, what's happening, and why.

THE COSTS OF TEACHER PENSIONS

During 2017, the most recent year for which we have comparable national data, states and school districts spent approximately $47 billion on teacher pension plans. Meanwhile, teachers and other educators were required to contribute another $22 billion of their own money.[5] Both of these figures have risen significantly over time.

Perhaps the best way to put these figures in context is to consider them in terms of actuarially required contribution rates.[6] That is, pensions typically are funded as a tax on labor. For every $100 a teacher earns in salary, they must contribute some percentage of their own money, and their employer (typically a district or state)[7] also must pay some additional percentage. For example, in 2001, in the wake of the stock market boom of the late 1990s, the average member contribution rate for state-run teacher pension plans was 5.2%, and the average employer contribution rate was 8.3%. To illustrate, for every $100 in salary, the teacher took home $94.80 and the employer would pay $108.30 in salaries and retirement.

Since then, pension plans have suffered from two recessions and states and school districts have been forced to increase contribution rates as a result. As of 2017, the average member contribution rate in teacher pension plans was 6.9%,[8] and the average employer contribution rate was 16.3%. Following the example above, the teacher's take-home pay for the same $100 in salary would fall to $93.10, while the employer's cost would rise to $116.30. Figure 2.1 shows how these rates have changed over time. While teachers may not see the effects of rising employer contribution rates, they may have noticed the cut in their take-home pay.

Figure 2.1. Actuarially Required Teacher Pension Contribution Rates, State Average

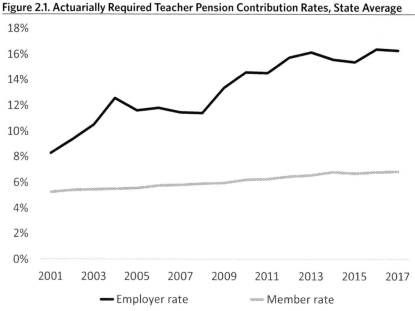

Source: Author's analysis of data from the Public Plans Database: publicplansdata.org

Unfortunately for teachers, rising employer contribution rates reflect a school district's cost to employ someone, not what an individual employee actually will receive in benefits. That's because the rising cost of teacher retirement systems is primarily a function of debt, in the form of unfunded liabilities. Worse, contribution rates have risen even as states have been cutting benefits, particularly for new members (Aubry & Crawford, 2017; Kan & Adelman, 2015). Teachers are paying more for diminished benefits.

The best way to visualize this is by examining how pension plans set contribution rates. Within traditional pension systems, we find two types of contributions: the amount of money that the plan's actuaries estimate it will need to pay out future benefits to members (called the "normal cost") and the cost of paying down any accumulated unfunded liabilities (called "amortization costs"). The normal cost is the amount of money a pension plan projects that it needs to contribute now to pay benefits in the future. The amortization cost is the amount required to pay down any accrued debt. Both costs are framed as a percentage of salary across all active employees participating in the plan.

If pension costs were rising because normal costs were rising, that would reflect an improvement in teacher benefits. But as Figure 2.2 shows, that's not what's happening. Today, amortization costs make up a bigger proportion of employer retirement costs than normal costs. As the graph shows, the average employer normal cost of teacher retirement benefits fell from about 6.2% of salary to slightly less than 5%, while amortization costs, a.k.a. debt costs, rose from an average of 2% of teacher salary to more than 11%. Going back to the example above, for every $100 school districts pay to teachers in the form of salary, they (or their state) must pay $16.30 toward the state-run teacher pension plans. Of that $16.30, $11.20 must go toward unfunded pension liabilities, and only $5.10 goes toward benefits for current teachers. To use a metaphor from personal finance, it's as if states failed to make sufficient payments on their credit cards, and now their interest costs have ballooned.

For comparison purposes, a 5% employer contribution rate would be considered mildly generous in the private sector. (Most experts recommend that workers save 12–15% of their salaries, including employer contributions, every year they work in order to secure a healthy retirement nest egg.) From an employer's perspective, the 5% normal cost in teacher pension plans is roughly equivalent to offering a 5% match on a 401(k) plan, which is more, but not much more, than the typical private-sector employer offers.[9] All employees covered under 401(k) plans with a 5% match would receive that amount in an individual, completely portable retirement account.

This is different from how benefits accrue under the defined benefit pension plans that are typical in public education. Because DB plans rely on formulas derived from salaries and years of experience, teachers receive very different amounts depending on their age, salary history, and how long they

Figure 2.2. Employer Contribution Rates to Teacher Pension Plans, by Type of Contribution

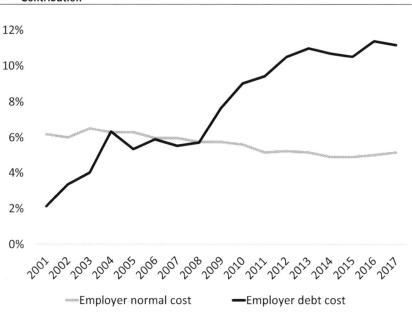

Source: Author's analysis of data from the Public Plans Database: publicplansdata.org

taught. Some teachers eventually will earn benefits worth far more than average, while many others will earn significantly less. Although the numbers vary by state, on average only about 15–20% of teachers remain for their entire career and truly maximize the promised pension (Aldeman & Robson, 2017).

Moreover, a substantial body of literature finds that teachers do not value $1 in benefit spending as much as they value $1 in base salaries. We see that prospective teachers are no more or less likely to enter the profession when teachers are asked to pay higher employee contribution rates, nor do early-career teachers change their behaviors to qualify for a pension (e.g., "vest" into the plan). In fact, when states and districts have enhanced pension plan formulas, sometimes at great expense, only a small fraction of long-serving veterans change their behaviors in response.[10] When other states have cut benefits or switched to alternative plan designs entirely, teacher retention patterns barely changed. At the back end, researchers have found that both pension plans and retiree health care plans push veteran teachers and principals out of schools and into retirement.[11] Those studies all look at the benefit provisions offered to teachers, but a study from Oregon found that the state pension plan's rising amortization costs caused teacher retention rates to decline.[12] In sum, pensions are not the dominant factor driving retention decisions for most teachers, and the current structures are not the most efficient use of limited resources.

TEACHER HEALTH CARE BENEFITS

The main difference in health care benefits offered in the public versus the private sector is the extent of coverage: Teachers are much more likely than employees in other fields to receive health care benefits, both while they're working and after they're retired.[13] This is a big discrepancy. Two-thirds of all employees in the private sector have access to medical-care benefits through their employer, whereas 99% of public schoolteachers do. Teachers are also far more likely than private-sector employees to have their health benefits extend beyond employment into retirement.

Teachers are also more likely than their private-sector peers to have access to supplemental health care benefits such as dental care (58% vs. 42%), vision care (36% vs. 23%), and prescription drug coverage (97% vs. 66%).

Among active workers, total medical care spending for individual plans are higher compared with those for private-sector workers, but the value of family plans is lower. Teachers also bear a slightly lower share of those costs than private-sector workers do, but the gaps are not large. Compared with private-sector workers, a larger share of teachers has their full medical premiums paid for by their employers (24% vs. 15%). For individual coverage, teachers receive a medical-care subsidy from their employers worth about $6,168 per year, or about $961 more than what private-sector workers receive, which is about 18% higher. Teachers themselves pay an average of $1,175 toward annual premiums, compared with $1,384 for private-sector employees.

For family plans, teachers contribute $257 more than nonteachers, school districts contribute about $600 less than private employers, and the total cost of the plans is actually a couple hundred dollars higher than for private-sector workers.

Another important difference is that teachers receive medical coverage for a full calendar year, even though they may work for only 10 months. About 18% of teachers earn income from a second or third job, but when they seek outside employment, teachers need not worry about health care coverage, a protection that not all workers have.

Adding up all these factors, the average active teacher receives health benefits that are better than those of employees in other sectors. Those differences are driven mainly by differences in coverage, not the generosity of the underlying benefits.

That coverage extends into retirement for two-thirds of public schoolteachers. For decades, public and private employers were able to offer retiree health benefits as part of employees' compensation packages without fully accounting for their cost. That began to change in the private sector in the mid-1980s, when new accounting rules forced companies to include the long-term liabilities of postemployment health care benefits on their balance sheets. With the change, companies were required to account for the projected expense of future promises and make those liabilities public, rather than just reporting the annual costs of paying for the benefits during a given year. Companies quickly decided that it made more sense to close the plans than to budget for their true cost. The share of large and midsized employers offering retiree health benefits fell from 45% in 1988 to 24% in 2017, Bureau of Labor Statistics data show. Smaller employers are even less likely to offer such benefits. Across all private-sector employers, just 15% of workers have access to employer-provided retiree health benefits.

For public-sector workers such as teachers, however, the numbers remain much higher. In 2017, 69% of public schoolteachers were employed in states or districts that offered retiree health benefits to workers under age 65, and 61% of teachers worked for an employer that offered health benefits even after age 65, when all Americans become eligible for Medicare. However, a change in accounting rules for state and local agencies was adopted in 2008, similar to that for the private sector, forcing state and local governments to publicly report long-term obligations that they had long ignored. Although we don't have good data disaggregated for teacher plans, 15 states, including large ones like Florida, New Jersey, and New York, have zero dollars set aside to pay for their retiree health care obligations. Nationwide, future projected health care costs for retirees are just 7% funded. California has a funded ratio of 0.2%, Connecticut, 1.0%, Pennsylvania, 1.6%, and Texas, 1.2%. Put simply, there is no money saved to cover 93% of the anticipated costs for retirees' health care benefits.

As with pension benefits, retiree health benefits were supposed to have been prefunded. If states had been responsible for setting aside the money they promised at the time they promised it, they wouldn't be in the deep hole they are in today. Instead, retiree health care obligations represent a fixed cost (and a potentially growing one, if health care costs continue to rise), which will hurt slow-growing states more than those with rapidly rising student enrollment.

That may make retiree health benefits especially vulnerable to budget pressures. Unlike pensions, which often have legal protections that restrict the changes states can make for existing workers and retirees, retiree health benefits have few protections. They could be on a budgetary chopping block at any time. Pensions may be where the bulk of the long-term cost pressures are, but policymakers may prefer reforming retiree health benefits for the more immediate cost savings. The next section tackles some options for policymakers who want to improve the efficiency of their spending while still providing teachers with secure and financially stable benefits.

POSSIBLE SOLUTIONS

The creeping costs of teacher benefits are playing out largely underneath the surface, away from higher-visibility fights about teacher pay, class sizes, charter schools, or other reform efforts (see the following section). But if policymakers don't pay attention, rising benefit costs will continue to cut into education budgets and force some hard choices. Halting these trends won't be easy, but there are potential solutions.

Perhaps the hardest problem to fix will be the $500 billion in unfunded pension liabilities. These debts reflect promises to current and future retirees, and strong legal protections, not to mention moral and political ones, block states from simply wiping them away, no matter how much of a financial burden they represent.

Still, states should start by curbing the accumulation of new pension debts. By closing their existing pension plans and enrolling future hires in different types of retirement plans that more closely link benefits to contributions, states at least can prevent the hole from becoming deeper. As one example, in 2012 Rhode Island closed its old defined benefit pension plan in favor of a hybrid plan combining a smaller pension and a defined contribution component, like the 401(k) plans more common in the private sector. While that change did not wipe away the state's debt, it did put Rhode Island on sounder financial footing going forward. Similarly, in 2011 Utah switched from a pure defined benefit plan to offering its teachers a choice between a hybrid plan and a defined contribution plan. The catch was that the state capped its contributions at 10% of salary under either plan, and over time the hybrid plan has faced rising unfunded liabilities that are eating up larger and larger shares of that 10%, whereas in the defined contribution plan, there are no unfunded liabilities and the entire 10% is going to workers.

As discussed above, many states are already offering their new employees pension plans with quite meager benefit formulas, the costs of which increasingly are borne by the workers themselves. Instead, states should enroll *future* workers into cost-neutral alternatives like defined contribution plans or "cash balance" plans, which provide worker benefits in terms of a guaranteed rate of return rather than the formulas traditional pension plans use.[14] Both of those options do a better job of providing all workers with secure, portable retirement benefits while capping employer retirement costs going forward.[15] At the very least, states could give teachers a choice of retirement plans, as Utah and several other states allow.

Even if the existing unfunded liabilities will not go away, states should still consider changing the entity that is responsible for paying down those obligations. In most states today, school districts are being asked to pay the costs of unfunded pension liabilities, even though it was state legislators and governors who created the plans, hired the actuaries to evaluate the plans, and ultimately set the benefit formulas and contribution rates. As such, states should bear the costs of unfunded liabilities and stop passing them on to local school districts.

In contrast to pensions, there are more immediate savings available on the health care side, where school districts should follow the lead of employers in other sectors. School districts tend to offer more generous health care packages than other employers, and they also tend to cover a higher share of the costs of those benefits. Asking teachers to pay a higher share would not be popular, but it would help increase transparency and encourage teachers to be active participants in keeping health care costs in check. Or, as the example of Miami-Dade illustrates in Chapter 4, districts may be able to reduce their costs by taking a more active role in health care decisions—or in the case of large districts, taking on the role of health care insurer entirely.

Much like the private sector has shifted away from offering pension plans with unpredictable costs, districts could shift their health care contributions to a more predictable allocation. Such a move would place a heavier burden on employees in the short term, but it potentially could help control health care costs over the long term if the end users, employees, had more of a financial stake in their own health care. At the very least, it could give employees a greater appreciation for how much their health care benefits actually cost and could create demand for broader cost reductions.

For their part, national teachers unions should stop opposing efforts to control health care costs, such as their role in resisting the "Cadillac tax" on high-cost health care plans. Higher-cost health care benefits do not necessarily produce better health outcomes, and reforms that would help limit the rise of health care costs would allow employers eventually to reinvest their savings into higher payrolls (Frakt, 2010; Furman, 2015). Such a step would require some long-term thinking on the part of union leaders, but curtailing costs in the short term would likely pay dividends for their members in the long run.

Current retiree health benefit plans should be on the chopping block entirely. As designed today, they are expensive, underfunded, and regressive, not to mention largely redundant of national programs like Obamacare and Medicare. Private-sector companies long ago decided that postemployment retirement benefits were unsustainable, once the true costs of those promises started to become apparent. State governments have been responding to their own, more recent budgetary awakening by enacting stricter eligibility requirements; it's not uncommon today to see states offering retiree health benefits but limiting eligibility to workers with 15, 20, or even 25 years of service. Yet that approach is regressive and unsustainable. While all teachers pay for these benefits, fewer and fewer workers are eligible to receive them. And the ones who are tend to be the highest-paid, most stable workers. At some point, a generation of teachers is likely to balk at paying for a benefit that is available only to a few long-serving members of their cohort.

Taxpayers also might recoil at the idea of spending more on education while seeing less and less of their investment actually make it into classrooms.

States are already coming to this realization. North Carolina, for example, recently announced that it would not offer retiree health benefits to state workers who begin their employment after January 2021. (This does not affect teachers, who are employed by their local districts.) The North Carolina model may sound draconian at first, but it's worth a second look, mainly due to the protections offered by Obamacare and Medicare. For retirees under age 65, the federal Affordable Care Act provides health care subsidies on a sliding scale based on income. In 2018, a two-member household earning less than $65,840, or 400% of the federal poverty level, qualified for assistance. That's more than the average, and even the median, teacher pension in most states. A retired teacher with no other sources of income would likely qualify for federal subsidies that would cover some or all of the costs of a basic health care plan.

The Obamacare exchanges are designed to be a bridge until workers qualify for Medicare at age 65, but many states and districts still provide benefits beyond that point. However, Medicare offers a reasonable floor of benefits open to all, and there's little public purpose accomplished by states or districts subsidizing benefits beyond that.[16] To put it bluntly, it no longer makes sense for states or districts to offer their own, less targeted plans when federal protections already cover the most vulnerable members of our society.

Tackling pension and health care benefits will not be politically popular, and politicians who try to take any of the steps outlined above should be prepared to face accusations that they are taking away teacher benefits. But brave politicians who want to leave a positive legacy should respond by walking through the numbers and explaining how current benefit structures are harming teachers in their state. They also should be prepared to grandfather in current workers and retirees as a way to transition to a new system. That would leave current unfunded liabilities largely intact, and smart leaders would come up with a plan for paying those down over time as well. But all sides must be prepared to compromise on these issues. Teachers may not know it, but their paychecks are being reduced due to rapidly rising benefit costs. Over time, governors and legislators who want to free up more discretionary dollars in their education budgets will have to tackle benefits. Those efforts not only will lead to more transparency on how education budgets are being spent, but also will lead to more dollars going into teachers' pockets.

SIDEBAR: HOW DO BENEFITS WORK IN CHARTER SCHOOLS?

The rise in teacher benefit costs has coincided with the rise in public charter schools, and some charter critics have been quick to link the two trends. In fact, some critics have argued, either implicitly or explicitly, that the rise in charter schools *caused* the rise in benefit costs. Although there is a kernel of truth to this argument, it would be easy to exaggerate just how much the two trends are linked.

Let's start with pension plans, by noting that most charter schoolteachers already participate in state teacher pension plans. In about half of the states with charter schools, laws *require* charter schools to participate in the state-run pension plans, and all participating employers pay the same contribution rates, regardless of whether or not they're charter schools (National Association of State Retirement Administrators, 2017). In states that let charters choose whether to participate, participation rates vary widely. A 2011 report for the Thomas B. Fordham Institute found that of the 16 states that allowed charter schools to choose, charter school participation ranged from 23% in Florida to 91% in California (National Association of State Retirement Administrators, 2017).

Another factor is that charter school enrollment, while growing, still represents only a small fraction of all students. That matters because pension contributions are determined on a *statewide* basis. So even if the charter sector gains market share in a particular city, that does not mean it will dramatically alter the dynamics of an entire state's pension plan.

To give a concrete example, consider the state of Michigan, where charter schools operated by education management organizations (EMOs) are exempt from participating in the statewide pension plan. From the perspective of the plan, it does not matter that charter schools enroll 53% of the students in the city of Detroit; all that matters is that approximately 7% of Michigan students are enrolled in schools operated by EMOs that do not participate in the pension plan (O'Keefe et al., 2017).

To continue with the Michigan example, the fact that EMOs can opt out of the statewide teacher pension plan does translate into higher contribution rates for traditional school districts, but those costs pale in comparison to the state's larger pension problems, where contributions toward unfunded liabilities have increased by 143% over the past 10 years. Now contrast that figure with the potential savings from forcing charters into the system.[17] In Michigan, participating school districts are required to pay 13.9% of each teacher's salary toward unfunded pension liabilities. If the state forced EMOs into the system, it potentially would broaden the total payroll base in the pension plan by the same 7%, meaning the employer contribution rate also could fall 7%, to 12.9% of salary. In Michigan and other states, the charter sector has played only a tiny role in the rising costs of teacher pensions.

Similar logic applies to charter schools and health care costs in traditional public school districts. District health care costs are a function of how many people districts employ and the coverage offered to those workers. In places where charter schools have gained market share at the expense of traditional school districts, it's possible that competition from charters is responsible for some portion of the rise in health care costs. But districts gain or lose students for a variety of reasons, including competition from charters, neighboring school districts, or private schools, not to mention birth rates and immigration, and it would be unfair to blame the charter sector if districts are unable to adjust the size of their workforce to better match the size of their student population.

Compared with traditional public school districts, charter schools also have made different choices about how to structure their benefit offerings in ways that avoid many of the problems faced by the traditional public school systems. For example, states and traditional public school districts are in their current situation because their benefit decisions are divorced from the cost of those benefits. That is, they have promised specific future benefits—through pension formulas, health care packages, or eligibility criteria for retiree benefits—that are not linked to the actual cost of those programs. Almost universally, states and districts have under-saved for those benefits, which has passed on the actual cost of those promises to future generations of teachers. In contrast, charter schools are much more likely to offer compensation packages where benefits are defined in terms of employer contributions. In those systems, there is no chance for the employer to under-save or over-promise, because the full cost of the benefits is paid up front. As a result, charter schools are able to devote larger portions of their compensation packages to higher base salaries, other personnel, and recruitment and retention incentives, instead of spending extra money on benefits.

NOTES

1. Districts also chose to hire many more teachers and administrative staff rather than raise teacher salaries. See, for example, https://www.edchoice.org/research/back-staffing-surge

2. Although this chapter is focused primarily on *state* pension plans, there are some large school districts, including New York City, Chicago, IL, and St. Louis and Kansas City, MO, that operate their own plans.

3. Here and other places, I'm referring to the pension plans covering public schoolteachers. Those plans often include other types of education employees, even as they're frequently called the "teacher" pension plan in any given state. In some states, teachers and other educators are grouped into a larger plan that includes other types of employees. The unfunded liabilities figure cited here relates only to the portion of state unfunded liabilities attributable to teachers and other education employees (Doherty et al., 2017)

4. See, for example, www.edchoice.org/research/back-staffing-surge

5. These figures come from the Boston College Center for Retirement Research's Public Plans Database, with a few adjustments. About half the plans in the database include educators and noneducators alike, so in order to get a closer estimate of the

education share, I applied weights based on the percentage of each plan's membership who are educators. For most states, the data run from fiscal year 2001 through fiscal year 2017, but data were not available for all states and all years, so these numbers represent an approximation rather than a precise figure.

6. The "actuarially required" contribution rate reflects the amount of money that plan actuaries estimate will need to be put into the system in the current year in order to pay for future benefits. Although some states do not pay the full amount of what their actuaries estimate they should contribute every year, for this chapter I use the term "contribution rate" to mean the plan's "actuarially required contribution rate."

7. Most states require school districts to pay the "employer" contribution rates, although a few states pay the full employer cost, and in a few other states it's split between districts and the state. For simplicity's sake, I refer to all of these arrangements as the "employer" contribution rate.

8. All of these figures exclude Social Security and any supplementary retirement plans, such as a 403(b) plan, that a teacher may voluntarily choose to join. For simplicity's sake, I use the term "teachers" throughout this chapter, but realistically the numbers also include other school support staff, principals, superintendents, and central office staff. As mentioned above, when educators are included in pension plans with noneducators, such as other state employees, I am referring only to the educator share.

9. My calculations from a large-scale analysis of more than 35,000 private-sector defined contribution plans suggest that about 25–30% of employers offer a 401(k) contribution of at least 5%. See Exhibit 2.3 at www.ici.org/pdf/ppr_14_dcplan _profile_401k.pdf

10. See overview of the research on pensions and retention effects at www .teacherpensions.org/blog/what-does-evidence-say-about-teacher-recruitment-retention -and-retirement

11. See www.ncbi.nlm.nih.gov/pmc/articles/PMC4258220

12. See www.bls.gov/osmr/research-papers/2016/pdf/ec160060.pdf

13. Throughout this section, I rely on data from the National Compensation Survey from the Bureau of Labor Statistics. For a more detailed overview, see www .educationnext.org/the-rising-cost-of-teachers%E2%80%99-health care

14. For more, see www.teacherpensions.org/resource/teacher-pension-plans -how-they-work-and-how-they-affect-recruitment-retention-and-equity

15. For more detail on how these plans work, see www.teacherpensions.org /resource/insufficient-how-state-pension-plans-leave-teachers-inadequate-retirement -savings

16. If employers want to continue offering their own supplemental benefits, they could sponsor health savings accounts for workers who have the means and want to save on their own for additional medical expenses not covered by Medicare.

17. This section looks merely at costs, but forcing charter schoolteachers into traditional teacher pension plans also would not be good for those workers. Due to relatively high mobility rates, charter schoolteachers typically would be better off in alternative plans more common in the charter sector. See, for example, www .teacherpensions.org/blog/are-pension-plans-better-charter-school-teachers

REFERENCES

Aldeman, C., & Robson, K. (2017, May 16). *Why most teachers get a bad deal on pensions*. Education Next. https://www.educationnext.org/why-most-teachers-get-bad-deal-pensions-state-plans-winners-losers

Aubry, J., & Crawford, C. (2017, January). *State and local pension reform since the financial crisis*. Center for Retirement Research at Boston College. https://crr.bc.edu/briefs/state-and-local-pension-reform-since-the-financial-crisis/

Doherty, K. M., Jacobs, S., & Lueken, M. F. (2017, February). *Lifting the pension fog*. www.nctq.org/dmsView/Lifting_the_Pension_Fog

Employer costs for employee compensation historical listing. (2020). www.bls.gov/web/ecec/ececqrtn.pd

Frakt, A. (2010, January 7). *Do premiums affect wages?* The Incidental Economist. theincidentaleconomist.com/premiums-wages

Furman, J. (2015, October 7). *Next steps for health care reform [Remarks at the Hamilton Project]*. https://www.hamiltonproject.org/assets/files/jason_furman_next_steps_health_care_reform_speech.pdf

Kan, L., & Aldeman, C. (2015, July 7). *Eating their young*. Teacherpensions.org.www.teacherpensions.org/resource/eating their-young

National Association of State Retirement Administrators. (2017, August). *State policies governing pension plan participation by charter school employees*. www.nasra.org/files/Compiled%20Resources/charterschoolpolicies.pdf

O'Keefe, B., Pennington, K., & Mead, S. (2017, January 30). *Michigan education policy fact base*. Bellwether Education Partners. bellwethereducation.org/sites/default/files/MI%20Slide%20Deck%20finalfinal%20w%20acknowledgements.pdf

U.S. Department of Education, National Center for Education Statistics. (2017, November). *Table 211.20: Average base salary for full-time teachers in public elementary and secondary schools, by highest degree earned and years of teaching experience: Selected years, 1990–91 through 2015–16*. nces.ed.gov/programs/digest/d17/tables/dt17_211.20.asp

CHAPTER 3

The Relationship Between School Funding and Student Outcomes

Adam Tyner

One of the odder and less enlightening education debates of the past quarter-century has been the dispute over "Does money matter?," as economist Gary Burtless put it in a 1996 volume. The dispute focused on the question of whether spending more dollars on schools led to better-educated students.

On one side were analysts who looked at a range of outcomes and noted that the relationship of spending to achievement seemed tepid. Most notably, economist Eric Hanushek wrote an influential series of articles spanning decades and casting doubt on the importance of focusing on school "inputs," including spending. On the other were scholars, like Burtless, who saw evidence that spending sometimes did seem to have a real impact on student outcomes.

While teachers unions, education school scholars, advocates, and litigators published cost studies and brought lawsuits that pressed for greater and more equitable spending, Burtless (1996) notes that Hanushek's view that there is little relationship between spending and student outcomes was then "the prevailing view among economists who study school resources and educational achievement" (p. 3). Noting that scores on the National Assessment of Educational Progress (NAEP) and the SAT had stagnated while per-pupil spending rose, the Cato Institute's Andrew Coulson was quoted in 2014 as saying that education data show that "changes in spending patterns have had no impact on performance" (Skorup, 2014).

To most Americans, the claim that money didn't matter to schools probably felt a little unreal. After all, most of us are inclined to believe that of course money makes a difference. Having more money allows us to buy better cars, pay for better houses, and afford nicer restaurants. So it would be surprising if more money didn't help schools improve.

The debate about whether money "matters" is in its 6th decade, but it is finally showing signs of petering out. While early studies sowed doubt about whether money really mattered, research has steadily accumulated that the early questioning of the importance of school funding should never have been convincing and that school funding has clear impacts on student performance, especially for the least advantaged students.

The rest of this volume is focused on the question of what schools do with their funding and how they can spend it better. But first, this chapter will unpack the debate over school funding and explain how a new wave of research has, in my view, settled these debates by demonstrating that having equitably funded schools is an important education policy objective. With this debate in our rearview mirror, we finally can move on to the more interesting—and perhaps more important—questions about what schools ought to do with all that money.

SOWING DOUBT ABOUT WHETHER MONEY MATTERS

The first salvo in this modern debate came from one of the most ambitious social science projects ever attempted, James Coleman's 1966 study of inequality in America's schools. Mandated by the Civil Rights Act of 1964, Coleman's study was unprecedented in its scope and dwarfs all but a handful of social research projects in the more than half a century that has followed. The Equality of Educational Opportunity project utilized data on more than half a million students, more than 40,000 teachers, and almost 4,000 administrators. The goal was to analyze the extent to which different factors contributed to student academic achievement, and Coleman's findings surprised him. Instead of school factors that he studied being the main drivers of student success and failure, Coleman found that peer and family factors were more important. Using the best statistical techniques available at the time, the study reported that the most important factors for student academic success were to be found in families, neighborhoods, and peer groups, not in teacher characteristics like years of experience, and not in school spending. Once Coleman controlled for student socioeconomic factors, "it appears that differences between schools account for only a small fraction of differences in pupil achievement" (Coleman, 1966, pp. 21–22).

Coleman's analysis, and many analyses that followed it, implicitly or explicitly relied on the idea of an "education production function." The idea of the production function is that student outcomes are based on certain inputs, including family background and school factors.

A typical version of the education production function looks like this:

Schooling outcomes = f(school resources, family background) + u

In this production function equation, the outcomes of schooling are dependent on school resources and family background, and the variable u, which signifies the "error" term, contains everything else. Although the reader reasonably may insist that factors such as peer effects or the student's own motivation and natural abilities play important roles as well, researchers typically have narrowed their focus to this more limited description of education "production."

As researchers utilized the education production function model, what transpired was a surprisingly robust debate about a pretty simple question. Following Coleman, hundreds of studies examined the relationship between school spending and student performance. Taking these studies into account, economist Eric Hanushek, a scholar who has been a pioneer in finding creative ways to put student outcome data to use (e.g., see Hanushek, 1971), authored the most influential reviews of this literature, which followed Coleman's conclusions as well. In a series of highly publicized studies, Hanushek (1989) reported that once family background was accounted for, school funding was not an important predictor of student success.

Over the course of numerous articles questioning the connection between funding and academic outcomes, Hanushek's goal became clear: Instead of focusing on school "inputs," policymakers ought to focus on the "outcomes"—student learning and well-being. Such a focus on outcomes over inputs fit the zeitgeist of the era, when reformers in numerous fields sought ways to make public services more efficient by reorienting accountability around clear performance targets, and the public was alarmed at stagnant student outcomes following the publication of A Nation at Risk. Hanushek sums up the input/output argument this way: "The commonly used input policies—such as lowering class sizes or tightening the requirements for teaching credentials—are almost certainly inferior to altered incentives within the schools" (Hanushek, 2003, p. F64).

While Hanushek lobbied for a focus on outputs over inputs, W. N. Grubb's The Money Myth, published in 2009, aimed to steer the conversation away from overall funding to more nuanced topics about how money was spent and what was going on in classrooms. For his part, Grubb explicitly rejects "the idea that 'money doesn't matter'" to school performance, calling the proposition "facile" and warning "fiscal conservatives and anti-taxers" not to take comfort in his arguments. Yet in the next moment, Grubb muddies the waters, declaring it a "myth" that "more money leads to improved outcomes, that the solution to any educational problem requires increased spending," and that lack of financial resources is behind most educational problems (p. xii). Although between 1971 and 2010, 28 state supreme courts required school finance reforms that led to more equal funding across districts, Grubb downplayed the potential effects of such reforms, arguing that people have already given up on the idea that court-induced spending changes could meaningfully improve equity.

Like Hanushek, Grubb was concerned that emphasizing a particular input, funding, was crowding out other necessary conversations about how money should be spent and which more specific resources—better prepared teachers, improved school climate—would make a difference to student learning. Yet however much he might protest it, calling the impact of school funding a "myth" (in the title of his book!) contributed to the idea that focusing on increasing inputs—especially in underserved schools—was at best a distraction from more important issues and at worst a waste of time.

Beyond Coleman's and Hanushek's empirical arguments and Grubb's theory-based aversion to a focus on school funding, a more commonsense argument that money doesn't matter to schools comes from simply observing student performance over the decades during which school funding has ballooned. Consider Figure 3.1, where a simple "eye test" shows that increases in spending have been greatly outpacing growth in academic achievement—measured by 4th-grade, 8th-grade, and 12th-grade scores on the NAEP. The figure shows that from 1990 to 2009, there was a 36% increase in inflation-adjusted spending. This sharp jump in per-pupil spending far exceeds the period's student performance increases, which range from –1% (12th-grade reading) to 9% (4th-grade math).[1]

Figure 3.1. NAEP Changes During a Time of Large Spending Increases

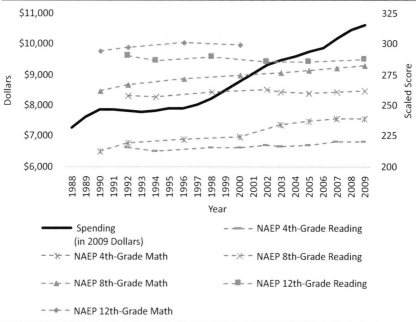

Note: Data on NAEP outcomes are from the NAEP Data Explorer and come with the following footnote for some data points: "Accommodations were not permitted for this assessment." I exclude 12th-grade math since the data are not comparable across this period. Data on school spending come from Revenues and Expenditures for Public Elementary and Secondary Education: School Year 2008–09 (Fiscal Year 2009). https://nces.ed.gov/pubs2011/expenditures/tables/table_06.asp

Looking at these data, a skeptic sensibly can ask, "If money matters to schools, why isn't student achievement keeping pace with these huge funding increases?"

PROBLEMS WITH THE DOUBTS

Yet over time, researchers found two key problems with these influential reviews of the research on this topic and with the proposition that additional spending does not make a difference to student outcomes.

First, it was never clear from Coleman's or Hanushek's analyses that there was *no* relationship between funding and student outcomes. Instead, most of the scholars raising these doubts argued merely that the connection between funding and outcomes was not as strong as expected; that funding was less important than other factors, such as student background; or that a focus on inputs was crowding out more important conversations about student outcomes.

Consider once more Figure 3.1, which shows that educational spending appears to be outpacing growth in student achievement. Of course, many other factors could be driving spending or student achievement up or down, including new costs, changing student populations, delayed impacts of new funding, or any number of other factors. But regardless of what else might be going on, the truth is that achievement generally *is* increasing as funding is going up, at least for elementary and middle school students.[2] Figure 3.1, with all but the essentially flat 12th-grade reading scores going up over time, demonstrates that the raw correlation over time between per-pupil funding and student achievement isn't negative, and it isn't zero; the correlation is positive.

This type of eye-test correlation is *not* a good way to find out whether "money matters," but this type of lay analysis bears relation to the hundreds of correlational studies on which the case was made that money didn't matter.

Hanushek was always careful to point out the data limitations of the studies on which his analyses were based, but he often pivoted from stating that the correlations were weak to implying that they didn't exist. Consider this typical quote from Hanushek's seminal study from 1989:

> Expenditure increases, if undertaken within the current institutional structure, are likely to be dissipated on reduced class sizes or indiscriminate raises in teacher salaries, with a result that growth in costs will almost surely exceed growth in student performance. (p. 50)

Although framed as an argument that more money would be wasteful, the statement does not dispute that more money would lead to "growth in student performance," only that the amount of growth in student outcomes would not be proportional to the spending increase. Presumably, this means that, say, a 10% increase in spending would not result in the same 10% increase in test scores or other student outcomes, arguably an exceedingly high bar for evaluating return on investment in schools.

A recent review of the effects of school funding on student outcomes notes that Hanushek finds a statistically significant positive effect of funding on student performance in more than a fourth of the studies he looked at, and just 7% of those studies showed significant negative results. Hanushek characterizes this as a wash and as suggestive evidence that funding doesn't make a difference. But in fact, "there are more than 10 times as many positive and significant studies than would be expected by random chance alone if the true effect were zero" (Jackson, 2018).

Coleman's and Hanushek's traditional analyses casting doubt on the importance of financial resources already suggested a link between funding and student outcomes.[3] Coleman's point was not that school funding made no difference, but that it made *less* of a difference than we might expect or than might be attributable to other factors, such as family background. Although occasionally making more definitive statements that most reviewers do not believe were justified by his findings,[4] Hanushek typically reminded readers that the data were limited and that such shortcomings might limit the possibility of identifying the impacts of the inputs. When researchers followed up on Hanushek's studies with more sophisticated meta-analysis methods, they found only stronger links between school funding and performance (Hedges et al., 1994).

The second main problem with this literature is the difficulty of disentangling the effects of family environment and school funding (Dewey et al., 2000). Recall the education production function, which describes education outcomes as a function of family background and school factors. If these two broad classes of "inputs"—family and school—were themselves unrelated, researchers could separate their effects more accurately. But, to the contrary, school funding in the United States has been largely a local affair, and this was even more true in the era when the early studies were conducted. With funding raised locally, richer families naturally sent their children to schools with more resources. Statistically, that means that fully separating the effect of school funding and family background is impossible using observational data of the kind analyzed in these studies. Since family background and school funding are themselves correlated, controlling for family background obscures and attenuates the actual relationship between school spending and student outcomes in a way that makes it *less* likely that an effect of school spending will be found.

Moreover, families exercise some choice over where their children attend school, and some families may be better at taking advantage of school resources, for example, by getting their child placed in a classroom with a more effective teacher or in an accelerated program. As Caroline Hoxby (2016) puts it, "Part of the apparent family effect was really a choose-effective -teachers effect" (p. 68). Thus, by controlling for family background, these early correlational studies attributed effects to families that were actually school inputs. While Coleman's original insight that family background and peers were perhaps as important as—or more important than—schools themselves may be true, none of this was evidence that school inputs did not matter at all. As economist Kirabo Jackson (2018) says in a recent review of this research, "Any claim that there is little evidence of a statistical link between school spending and student outcomes is demonstrably false."

ISOLATING THE IMPACT OF SCHOOL SPENDING

Although the early studies on the impact of school funding on academic outcomes tended to mix effects of family background and school inputs together in ways that underestimated the effect of school funding, later studies have more successfully isolated the impact of funding itself. These studies have identified consistent positive effects of better-funded schools, with disproportionate positive impact on students from low-income families. Although many of these studies are narrowly designed to conclusively determine whether there is a positive effect of new funding on student outcomes, a downside to this approach is that it can limit the applicability of these studies to other contexts, a topic to which we will return in the conclusion to this chapter.

To isolate the impact of funding, completely separating the effect from family background and other factors, researchers often use clever techniques that leverage changes in funding that are plausibly random and unrelated to other factors being studied. For example, a number of studies have looked at places where budget referenda passed or failed by thin margins, under the assumption that places where the vote margin was close to the cutoff are highly similar and that differences in student outcomes between such locations can be attributed to the increased funding from the passage of the referenda (Abott et al., 2019; Baron, 2019; Kogan et al., 2017; Lee & Polachek, 2014; Rauscher, 2020). Another strategy has been to use the "shock" of court-imposed school finance reforms as a way to study the impact of funding.[5] Although Grubb had given up on the idea that court-imposed school finance reforms would make a difference, these recent studies show that school finance reforms that were initiated through litigation have had measurable positive impacts on funding and student outcomes, while narrowing funding and achievement gaps across groups (Biasi, 2015; Brunner et al., 2018; Candelaria & Shores, 2019; Card & Payne, 2002; Jackson et al., 2015; Johnson & Jackson, 2018; Lafortune et al., 2018; Papke, 2008).

These newer studies isolate the impact of funding changes and find effects of increased funding on a range of student outcomes, including reading and math scores, SAT scores, high school graduation, and a variety of other adult outcomes related to income and poverty.[6] The cumulative results are unambiguous: Of the 33 studies reviewed by Jackson (2018), just eight report no effect, although some studies report positive effects for some outcomes and no effect for others.[7]

But more important, unlike the earlier studies, not a single study using these more rigorous research methods reports a negative effect of school funding on any of the student outcomes analyzed. If there really was no effect of funding on student outcomes, we would expect only a small proportion to have statistically significant results, instead of the overwhelming majority.[8] And of those with significant results, we would expect that around half would show a *negative* effect. In fact, the vast majority of these studies with the most rigorous research designs show positive, statistically significant effects of money on school performance, and none shows a negative and statistically significant effect.

Further, most of this new generation of studies that demonstrate that money matters to schools also show that when funding went up, specific inputs that make a difference to school performance increased as well. For example, a study of school finance reforms in Michigan showed that increased funding led to lowered class sizes, higher teacher salaries, and a lower student-to-administrator ratio.[9] Since some inputs have been shown to have strong effects on student outcomes, it makes sense that when new funds increase or improve those inputs, school performance increases will follow.

Whether it should ever have been open, in light of these numerous rigorous studies, the case that "money matters" is now closed.

HOW MUCH DOES SPENDING MATTER?

If, after all these decades, the debate about whether financial resources matter to school performance has been settled, what we have learned that is of use to administrators and policymakers is, unfortunately, quite limited. That's because the question of whether spending makes a difference to student outcomes is nebulous at best. Typically, what policymakers and administrators need to know is not whether money makes a difference, but what the relationship between money and school performance looks like—and what uses of money make what kind of differences in performance.

Consider the relationships between spending and student performance depicted in Figure 3.2. In each case, there is a *consistent positive relationship* between per-pupil spending and student learning. But to make optimal policies, policymakers must understand whether the effect of additional spending is large (upper left) or smaller (upper right), has diminishing returns (lower left), or applies differently to different groups (lower right).

Figure 3.2. Visualizations of Potential Curves Complicating the Question "Does Spending Matter?"

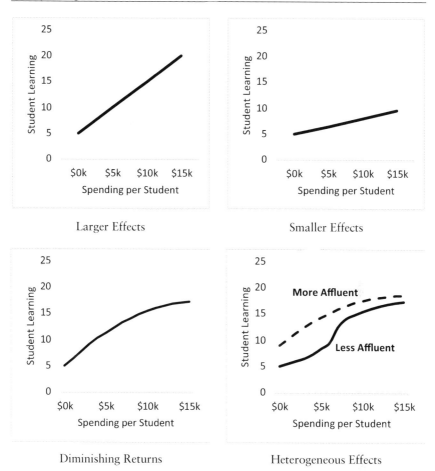

Yet spending will not influence all student outcomes equally. Imagine that the Y axis in Figure 3.2 isn't the abstract concept of "student learning" but something more specific, like "student reading ability" or "algebra test scores." Even before looking at any empirical studies, it is hard to imagine that the curve would not look quite different depending on the outcome of interest.

And even complete understanding of the relationship between spending and specific student outcomes is really not enough, since policymakers and administrators typically are confronted with specific questions about particular inputs. In some cases, the question may be about general funding levels, but more often a decision must be made about a specific input, such as teacher salaries, spending on technology, or adding teaching assistants to classrooms with special-needs students. The relationship between spending and student learning will fluctuate greatly depending on how the money is spent. The execution of policies makes a big difference, too, and we can imagine that the relationship between spending and student learning will vary within each spending category as well. If the technology budget goes to highly effective software or to hardware that soon will be obsolete, we can imagine that the impact curve will differ accordingly. What's more, these types of spending likely interact, such as when teacher professional development goes together with a new technological tool or when districts develop similar programs that compete with one another.

Unfortunately, the information that we typically get about how much a given amount of spending influences a student outcome is oversimplified and ultimately not too helpful to policymakers and practitioners. A 2018 national study on the effects of increased spending on student outcomes reported that a $1,000 increase in annual per-pupil spending that was carried out for 10 years in low-income school districts raised math and reading test scores by 0.12 to 0.24 standard deviations (Lafortune et al., 2018). Although this study finds that schools generally used the funds to increase instructional spending, reduce class sizes, and effect new capital outlays, it is unable to say which of these inputs was most responsible for the gains, let alone provide information about what a given district, with its particular circumstances, ought to do. And since there are likely to be diminishing returns to funding, this average effect in under-resourced schools probably will not apply to schools that are already spending more. At the same time, districts that were spending even less may see even larger gains, although many other factors could influence these effects as well.

At the school and district level, *your mileage will vary.*

TO WHOM DOES SPENDING MATTER?

Since the effects of spending differ according to the context, it should be no surprise that research consistently finds larger effects of increased spending in places with lots of traditionally disadvantaged students. Not only do students in poverty and those coming from historically oppressed minority groups often face additional challenges, and thus educating them requires greater resources, but—at least in the past—these students also have disproportionately attended schools that spent *less* per student (see Figure 3.3).[10]

A number of studies have broken out the effects of additional funding by student socioeconomic status and found that poorer students benefit more from funding than students from higher income families. For example, in a multi-state study, researchers looking at effects of tax increases for school spending didn't find clear evidence when they included all of a state's

Figure 3.3. Closing Funding Gaps Over Time

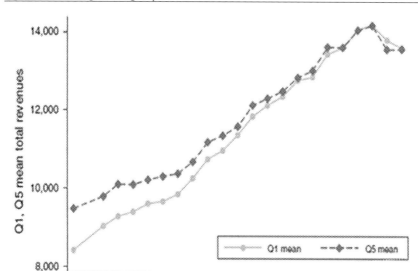

Note: Figure from Lafortune, J., Rothstein, J., & Whitmore Schanzenbach, D. (2018, April). School finance reform and the distribution of student achievement. *American Economic Journal: Applied Economics*, 10(2), 1–26. They note that the "highest (lowest) income districts are those in the top (bottom) 20% of their states' district-level distributions of mean household income in 1990, and are labeled as 'Q5' and 'Q1,' respectively. . . . Revenues are expressed in real 2013 dollars. Districts are averaged within states, weighting by log district enrollment; states are then averaged without weights. Hawaii and the District of Columbia are excluded" (p. 2). Copyright American Economic Association; reproduced with permission of the *American Economic Journal: Applied Economics*.

districts in their sample, but they found clear jumps in test scores in higher-poverty districts that raised taxes and increased school spending (Abott et al., 2019).[11] A national study of school finance reforms found small, statistically insignificant effects of additional funding on students from wealthier families, but an increase in achievement comparable to half an additional year of schooling over the course of 12 years of education for higher-poverty students (Jackson et al., 2015). The same study also found disproportionate impacts on poorer students for high school graduation, adult wages, and family income; the effect on high school graduation for low-income students was four times the effect for higher-income students, while a 10% increase in school funding for people from low-income families led to substantial gains in adult wages and adult family income, but no statistically significant effect for higher-income folks.

WHY ISN'T TITLE I FUNDING MORE EFFECTIVE?

Interestingly, while poor students benefit the most from additional spending, studies of Title I spending, which is federal money targeted specifically at poor students, have not consistently shown that the additional funding has been effective. Many studies have shown null results (Matsudaira et al., 2012; van der Klaauw, 2008; Weinstein et al., 2009), although two studies have shown at least some positive results of Title I spending on student outcomes (Cascio et al., 2013; Johnson, 2015). If poor students really benefit the most from increased funding, why isn't the largest federal program supplying funds to poor students showing clearer impacts?

The answer may be that increased Title I money, oddly, doesn't always result in additional money for schools. In multiple studies of Title I impacts, the scholars note that when federal Title I money began to flow, local sources of funding dried up, resulting in negligible additional funds for needy students (van der Klaauw, 2008). An assessment of how local funding reacts to Title I funding found that by the 3rd year following Title I funding increases, there was no statistically significant difference in net funding as a result of Title I "due to local government reactions countering the effects of Title I" (Gordon, 2004, p. 1790).[12]

Since funding disparities have narrowed considerably over time (see Figure 3.3), it is possible that current funding increases for poor students would have less of an impact than they have historically. Many of the impacts researchers have estimated in recent years come from changes made as far back as the 1970s, when national per-pupil spending was much lower than it is today. With much greater spending on schools in more recent years, it is reasonable to question whether new outlays, targeted at the neediest students or not, would get as much bang for the buck as recent studies have estimated.

TOWARD ACADEMIC RETURN ON INVESTMENT

As an influential review of this literature from 2018 put it, "The question of whether money matters is essentially settled" (Jackson, 2018, p. 14). The impact of greater funding is especially clear when it comes to schools that are underfunded or serve those tudents who are most disadvantaged. The time has passed when one plausibly could argue that equalizing inputs—or increasing them when they are low—isn't an important factor in improving schools.

This suggests that rather than continuing to debate this question, policymakers and advocates need to both demand that disadvantaged students have access to equitably funded schools and pivot to more nuanced questions like those raised by Grubb: How can we eliminate waste in the system?

How can we make every dollar count? Conveniently, you are already holding a book that tackles these questions head-on.

We must push forward with research on spending money more wisely by putting it to its best uses, because there is ample evidence that money is not optimally spent. Some large new outlays have gone up in smoke, being spent on things that have little connection with student learning, for example, shoring up pensions, as explained in Chapter 2. In other cases, blindly throwing money at the problem has been the main improvement strategy, as Chapter 9 explains often has been the case with special education programs.

More broadly, policymakers, administrators, and teachers must view programming from a more holistic and sophisticated perspective that assesses the impact of a program, estimates all the costs, and evaluates potential alternatives. Answering whether a given program "works," that is, has a "statistically significant impact," is not enough. Taking into account both the magnitude of the effect and the costs enables us to estimate what sometimes is called "academic return on investment" (AROI) for different expenditures. Thankfully, there has been recent movement in this direction. At the national level, the Institute of Education Sciences has begun to take into account, when evaluating research proposals, whether a cost analysis is included, and the U.S. Department of Education is training researchers how to evaluate the costs and benefits of programs (Sparks, 2019).

Then, to make a decision, the alternatives to the policy or program must be understood as well. Once estimates of the AROI of various inputs are available, it is possible for leaders to make an informed decision. In Chapter 5, Marguerite Roza suggests that a "would you rather" test is a useful way for stakeholders to think about competing alternatives.[13]

Researchers must be willing to get into the weeds of local conditions and help answer these questions. Many quantitative researchers seem hesitant to shoulder this burden because they worry that studies lacking plausibly experimental variation in the input or program are not truly "causal," and that it is therefore irresponsible to suggest that an input has a causal impact absent these rare circumstances. Yet this worry itself carries two big problems. First, however important it is that a study shows true causality—and it is obviously important—decisionmakers on the ground must worry about the applicability (or "generalizability") to their context at least as much as the purity of the causal claim.[14] Studies that cannot be applied to the circumstances faced by practitioners and administrators are of much less value on the ground, even if researchers are highly confident that they have identified a bulletproof causal effect. Second, the people responsible for making decisions about school funding, and about which inputs merit investment, have no choice but to make decisions, regardless of the quality of information on the topic. (Retaining the status quo is a decision as well.) If researchers focus only on contexts where they can employ the most powerful class of research designs, those making decisions about policies will be left with much less useful information and consequently will make suboptimal decisions.

After all of the studies proving that funding generally makes a difference to schools, a researcher helping a district evaluate alternatives among inputs, programs, or strategies is likely doing work with far greater impact than yet another study using some clever source of exogenous variation to once again "prove" that "money matters."

Funders have a role here as well. Foundations and philanthropists can dedicate resources to organizations working within the EROI framework to help decisionmakers make the best use of limited resources. If certain academic disciplines incentivize the development of studies with clever research designs over those that will help policymakers and practitioners make the best decisions, private funders can create countervailing pressures that guide the brightest quantitative researchers toward more applicable research questions.

Now that we know that money matters, we all have a responsibility to make sure that the education of underserved students is properly funded and that funds are going to their best possible uses.

NOTES

1. Cato Institute analyst Andrew Coulson used similar comparisons over the years, including a state-by-state analysis of school spending and SAT score trends. See Coulson (2014).

2. Jackson et al. (2015), responding to Hanushek's claim of little academic improvement in recent decades, provide a review of research on other recent progress, much of which disproportionately benefits traditionally disadvantaged students. Such positive trends include higher test scores, declining dropout rates, and increased postsecondary enrollment rates.

3. Jackson (2018) argued that Hanushek had already found a link between funding and performance. Jackson says that "if school spending and student outcomes were unrelated, then 2.5% of studies should be significant and positive and 2.5% should be significant and negative (with a two sided p-value of less than 0.05). Hanushek (2003) finds that 27% of these early studies were statistically significant and positive while 7% were significant and negative—there are more than 10 times as many positive and significant studies than would be expected by random chance alone if the true effect were zero." Hedges et al. (1994) perform a meta-analysis on a similar set of studies to those Hanushek (1989) analyzed and also find evidence of a correlation.

4. For example, "Simply providing more funding or a different distribution of funding is unlikely to improve student achievement" (Hanushek, 1997, p. 153).

5. For a discussion of school finance reforms during this period, see Jackson et al. (2015). The assumption is that courts rule in ways that generally are disconnected from the context of day-to-day funding and other related factors. Therefore, a court-imposed school finance reform is like a random "exogenous shock," and the resulting funding increases do not suffer from the biases inherent in comparing just

performance and funding across districts and states, as many of the early observational studies did. Still, since court decisions are not completely exogenous to social context, the validity of this assumption is debatable.

6. See Jackson (2018, Table 1) and Barnum (2019). In some of these studies, the researchers studied multiple outcomes or outcomes for multiple student subgroups, but not all effects were positive and statistically significant.

7. An example of a study that found some positive effects and some null effects is Lee and Polachek (2014), which reported that "increases in school expenditures reduce dropout rates but have limited effects on student test scores."

8. Unfortunately, "publication bias" ensures that many null findings are not published, so it is not impossible that reports about a null relationship would contain more statistically significant findings than otherwise should be expected. Still, the fact that Jackson (2018) reports that significant positive results outnumber significant negative results 25 to 0 should be interpreted as strong evidence that the effect is positive.

9. See Hyman (2017). Of course, the researchers were able to measure only these tangible inputs, and it is possible that the increased funding led to unobserved changes in the schools, such as new curricula, additional professional development opportunities for teachers, altered hiring practices, changed leadership, or other factors that may have both resulted from the new funding and influenced student outcomes.

10. Darling-Hammond (2013, p. 79) says, "In most states there is at least a three-to-one ratio between per pupil spending in the richest and poorest districts."

11. This study did not find clear effects of spending on graduation rates, although data limitations may have prevented the researchers from finding anything definitive.

12. Although federal law requires that Title I funds "supplement, not supplant" local funds, this requirement applies to the distribution of funds across schools, not to total funding in the district, which localities can still change. See Gordon (2004).

13. Still, even the most developed estimates of AROI will not definitively solve these issues because context matters, and to the extent that empirical research is always bound to contexts (e.g., Tennessee public school districts in the 1980s; U.S. middle school averages from the 1970s), study results can never completely dictate spending patterns.

14. Researchers sometimes call this the trade-off between "internal validity" (causality) and "external validity" (generalizability).

REFERENCES

Abott, C., Kogan, V., Lavertu, S., & Peskowitz, Z. (2019, May). *School district operational spending and student outcomes: Evidence from tax elections in seven states* (EdWorkingPaper No. 19-25). Annenberg Institute at Brown University. edworkingpapers.com/sites/default/files/ai19-25.pdf

Barnum, M. (2019, August 13). *4 new studies bolster the case: More money for schools helps low-income students.* Chalkbeat. https://chalkbeat.org/posts /us/2019/08/13/school-funding-spending-money-matter-latest-research-studies

Baron, E. (2019, August 1). *School spending and student outcomes: Evidence from revenue limit elections in Wisconsin.* Florida State University. papers.ssrn.com /sol3/papers.cfm?abstract_id=3430766

Biasi, B. (2015). *School finance equalization and intergenerational mobility: Does equal spending lead to equal opportunities?* [Working paper]. Russell Sage Foundation. www.russellsage.org/sites/all/files/conferences/Biasi_Draft.pdf

Brunner, E., Hyman, J., & Ju, A. (2018). School finance reforms, teachers' unions, and the allocation of school resources. *Review of Economics and Statistics*, pp. 1–47. www.mitpressjournals.org/doi/abs/10.1162/rest_a_00828

Burtless, G. (1996). *Does money matter? The effect of school resources on student achievement and adult success.* Brookings Institution Press.

Candelaria, C., & Shores, K. (2019, June 13). Court-ordered finance reforms in the adequacy era: Heterogeneous causal effects and sensitivity. *Education Finance and Policy, 14*(1), 31–60. doi.org/10.1162/edfp_a_00236

Card, D., & Payne, A. (2002, January 1). School finance reform, the distribution of school spending, and the distribution of student test scores. *Journal of Public Economics, 83*(1), 49–82. doi.org/10.1016/S0047-2727(00)00177-8

Cascio, E., Gordon, N., & Reber, S. (2013). Local responses to federal grants: Evidence from the introduction of Title I in the south. *American Economic Journal: Economic Policy, 5*(3), 126–159.

Coleman, J. (1966). *Equality of educational opportunity.* U.S. Department of Health, Education, and Welfare, Office of Education.

Coulson, A. (2014). State education trends: Academic performance and spending over the past 40 years. *Cato Institute Policy Analysis*, No. 746.

Darling-Hammond, L. (2013). Inequality and school resources. In P. L. Carter & K. G. Welner (Eds.), *Closing the opportunity gap: What America must do to give every child an even chance* (pp. 77–97). Oxford University Press.

Dewey, J., Husted, T., & Kenny, L. (2000, February 1). The ineffectiveness of school inputs: A product of misspecification? *Economics of Education Review, 19*(1), 27–45. doi.org/10.1016/S0272-7757(99)00015-1

Gordon, N. (2004). Do federal grants boost school spending? Evidence from Title I. *Journal of Public Economics, 88*(9–10), 1771–1792.

Grubb, W. N. (2009). *The money myth: School resources, outcomes, and equity.* Russell Sage Foundation.

Hanushek, E. A. (1971). Teacher characteristics and gains in student achievement: Estimation using micro data. *American Economic Review, 61*(2), 280–288.

Hanushek, E. A. (1989). The impact of differential expenditures on school performance. *Educational Researcher, 18*(4), 45–62.

Hanushek, E. A. (1997). Assessing the effects of school resources on student performance: An update. *Educational Evaluation and Policy Analysis, 19*(2), 141–164.

Hanushek, E. A. (2003). The failure of input-based schooling policies. *The Economic Journal, 113*(485), F64–F98.

Hedges, L., Laine, R., & Greenwald, R. (1994, April 1). An exchange: Part I: Does money matter? A meta-analysis of studies of the effects of differential school inputs on student outcomes. *Educational Researcher, 23*(3), 5–14. doi.org/10 .3102/0013189X023003005

Hoxby, C. (2016). The immensity of the Coleman data project: Gaining clarity on the report's flaws will improve future research. *Education Next, 16*(2), 64–70.

Hyman, J. (2017, November). Does money matter in the long run? Effects of school spending on educational attainment. *American Economic Journal: Economic Policy, 9*(4), 256–280.

Jackson, C. K. (2018, December). *Does school spending matter? The new literature on an old question* [Working paper]. National Bureau of Economic Research. doi.org/10.3386/w25368

Jackson, C. K., Johnson, R., & Persico, C. (2015). The effects of school spending on educational and economic outcomes: Evidence from school finance reforms. *The Quarterly Journal of Economics, 131*(1), 157–218.

Johnson, R. (2015, December 1). Follow the money: School spending from Title I to adult earnings. *The Russell Sage Foundation Journal of the Social Sciences, 1*(3), 50–76. doi.org/10.7758/RSF.2015.1.3.03

Johnson, R., & Jackson, C. K. (2018, June). *Reducing inequality through dynamic complementarity: Evidence from Head Start and public-school spending* [Working paper]. National Bureau of Economic Research. doi.org/10.3386/w23489

Kogan, V., Lavertu, S., & Peskowitz, Z. (2017). Direct democracy and administrative disruption. *Journal of Public Administration Research and Theory, 27*(3), 381–399.

Lafortune, J., Rothstein, J., & Whitmore Schanzenbach, D. (2018, April). School finance reform and the distribution of student achievement. *American Economic Journal: Applied Economics, 10*(2), 1–26. doi.org/10.1257/app.20160567

Lee, K., & Polachek, S. (2014, April 5). *Do school budgets matter? The effect of budget referenda on student performance* [SSRN scholarly paper]. Social Science Research Network. papers.ssrn.com/abstract=2420701

Matsudaira, J., Hosek, A., & Walsh, E. (2012). An integrated assessment of the effects of Title I on school behavior, resources, and student achievement. *Economics of Education Review, 31*(3), 1–14. doi.org/10.1016/j.econedurev.2012.01.002

Papke, L. (2008). The effects of changes in Michigan's school finance system. *Public Finance Review, 36*(4), 456–474.

Rauscher, E. (2020). Delayed benefits: Effects of California school district bond elections on achievement by socioeconomic status. *Sociology of Education, 93*(2), 110–131. doi.org/10.1177/0038040719892577

Skorup, J. (2014, April 10). *Michigan school funding up, results flat*. Michigan Capital Confidential. www.michigancapitolconfidential.com/school-spending-up-results-flat

Sparks, S. D. (2019, April 9). *More education studies look at cost-effectiveness*. Education Week. www.edweek.org/ew/articles/2019/04/10/more-education-studies-look-at-cost-effectiveness.html

van der Klaauw, W. (2008). Breaking the link between poverty and low student achievement: An evaluation of Title I. *Journal of Econometrics, 142*(2), 731–756. doi.org/10.1016/j.jeconom.2007.05.007

Weinstein, M., Stiefel, L., Schwartz, A., & Chalico, L. (2009). *Does Title I increase spending and improve performance? Evidence from New York City* (Working Paper No. 09-09). Institute for Education and Social Policy. eric.ed.gov/?id=ED556781

Part II

THE WAY FORWARD

CHAPTER 4

Schools and Systems That Are Getting More Bang for Their Buck

Michael Q. McShane

Ask almost any educator and they'll tell you that they "stretch the school dollar." It's a miracle they can even keep the doors open with how little money they get. Heck, ask anyone managing any enterprise and they'll tell you that they could use more funding, more staff, and more support. 'Twas ever thus.

But some education organizations really do try to rethink what they do and find demonstrable and replicable efficiencies. They eschew platitudes, ask hard questions, and hold themselves accountable for the financial health of their organizations.

These organizations exist in both the public and private sectors. They include some traditional public schools and districts, as well as charter schools that stretch the school dollar. Private schools do so, too. Perhaps surprisingly, the lessons that they learn can transfer across sectors and can help schools in very different circumstances to improve their efficiency and effectiveness.

To illustrate, this chapter will highlight three school networks. The Miami-Dade school district is a traditional public school district, one of the largest in the nation. The Arizona Math and Science Charter Schools are a network of high-performing charter schools in Tucson and Phoenix. And Seton Education Partners works with a network of Catholic schools across the country.

MIAMI-DADE COUNTY PUBLIC SCHOOLS: BUCKING THE STAFFING SURGE

The Miami-Dade County Public Schools is the fourth-largest district in the nation, educating more than 350,000 students. It has a larger pupil population than 13 states and the District of Columbia. When comparing current spending, the largest district in the country, New York City, spends almost $24,000 per student. The second-largest, Los Angeles, spends just over $13,000 per student. The third, Chicago, spends over $13,400. Miami spends $8,938 (U.S. Census Bureau, 2016). According to Payscale.com (2019), the cost of living is 50% lower in Miami than in New York, 20% lower than in Los Angeles, and 7% lower than in Chicago, meaning that even adjusting for cost of living, Miami spends far less per student than any of the three larger districts. Part of the way it's done this has been by bucking the nationwide trend of employing more teaching and nonteaching staff.

Dr. Ben Scafidi of Kennesaw State University has documented this school "staffing surge" for several years now (Scafidi, 2017). By comparing changes in K–12 enrollment with changes in the number of teachers and nonteaching staff, he has documented the enormous growth in personnel in school districts. If you stretch the timeline back to 1950, the student population nationwide has grown 100% (i.e., it has doubled), but the total number of school personnel has grown 381%. When Scafidi looked at that personnel number and divided it into teachers and nonteachers, he found that although the number of teachers grew 243% during that time, nonteaching staff grew 709%. One may argue that looking back to 1950 is inappropriate because the student population today is much more diverse and more likely to include students with special needs who need more individualized attention. When Scafidi (2017) concentrated on just 1992 to 2015, however, he found that the student population grew 19%, but the number of teachers grew 28%, and all other staff grew 45%.

I asked Dr. Scafidi to run the numbers for Miami-Dade and for Florida to see whether they kept up with this trend or bucked it. Looking at the United States as a whole from fiscal year 1994 to 2017, Scafidi estimated that the student population grew 16%, while the number of teachers grew 27%, and all other staff grew 51%. In Florida, the number of students grew 38%, while the number of teachers rose 69%, and all other staff went up 43%. In Miami-Dade, the number of students rose 16%, the number of teachers 35%, and all other staff 18%.[1] Figure 4.1 displays these data in graphic form.

At a time when public education's nonteaching staff grew nationally at a rate more than three times the rate of increase in the pupil population, Miami kept them growing in tandem. Although the number of teachers rose more than the number of students, when combining total staff, Miami's growth was 1.6 times student growth, while nationwide it was 2.4 times.

The financial data back this up. To quantify a district's administrative efficiency, Florida's Educational Funding Accountability Act requires districts to report administrative expenses and converts them into a measure of funds per full-time-equivalent (FTE) staff member. These figures are calculated for both general revenue funds and special revenue funds that districts spend. In both cases, Miami-Dade spends below the state average. With respect to

Figure 4.1. Percentage Growth in Students, Teachers, and Nonteaching Staff, 1994–2017

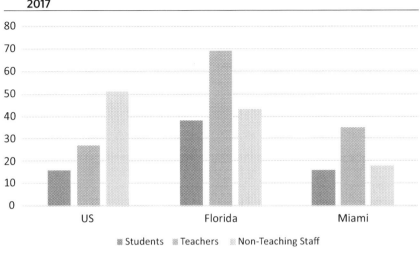

Source: Calculations by Dr. Ben Scafidi.

general funds, Miami-Dade spends $535.44 per FTE, while the state averages $572.35. With respect to special revenue funds, it spends $34.86 per FTE compared with the state's average of $35.44 (Florida Department of Education, 2019).

It does not appear that this relative parsimony comes at the expense of student achievement. Miami-Dade participates in the Trial Urban District Assessments (TUDA), the city-centric administration of the NAEP exam. In 2019, it dramatically outperformed the large-city average in 4th-grade reading (Miami scored an average of 225 scale-score points, while the large-city average was 212) and math (Miami scored an average of 246 scale-score points, while the large-city average was 235). In 8th-grade reading, Miami also outperformed national averages, although by a smaller margin (262 for Miami versus a large-city average of 255), and scored at the average for large cities in 8th-grade math (with 276 scale-score points for Miami and 274 for large cities, results that are not statistically different). In terms of changes over time, from 2009 to 2019 (as far back as consistent NAEP TUDA numbers go for Miami), the district has grown in 4th-grade math and reading by 10 and 4 scale-score points, respectively. It grew three points in 8th-grade math and remained stagnant in reading.

When compared with other large cities, Miami-Dade tends to end up near the top. In 2019, NAEP identified no districts (among TUDA participants) that outperformed it in 4th-grade reading, four districts with performance that wasn't significantly different, and 22 that scored below it. In

4th-grade math, NAEP identified no TUDA districts that scored higher than Miami-Dade, two that were about the same, and 24 that scored below it. In 8th-grade reading, NAEP again identified no districts that scored higher than Miami-Dade, four that were about the same, and 22 that performed below it. In 8th-grade math, NAEP identified four districts that performed better than Miami-Dade, eight that were similar, and 14 that performed below.

How did Miami-Dade do this?

Much can be attributed to the district's self-described "recession battle-hardened superintendent" Alberto Carvalho, who took the reins in Miami-Dade in 2008 and spent his first few years coping with the effects of the Great Recession. Where many school districts floundered, Carvalho believes Miami-Dade "turned that crisis into a profoundly transformative opportunity."[2]

Miami-Dade cut administrative staff by 55%. It shuttered one of two central office buildings because there was no staff to fill it. Many of those individuals were educators and were moved back to schools to work more directly with students. Others were simply laid off. The superintendent instituted a "zero-based, value-based budget" process that went line by line through spending and analyzed how every employee and program affected student learning. Even today, he admits that "adding a position to our budget is hard," as tough questions will be asked as to whether that job can be done by existing staff, solved by technology, or outsourced to a private provider.

Carvalho stresses that this was "not austerity, but cost reduction and realignment." He and his staff renegotiated contracts with vendors, refinanced existing debt, and, perhaps most significantly, took the operation of their health care system into their own hands.

For several reasons, south Florida is home to some of the largest and fastest rising health care expenses in the nation. The Miami-Dade district has nothing to do with the area's aging population or high rates of Medicare and Medicaid fraud but must deal with them nonetheless.

In response to double-digit annual cost increases for health insurance, the school system moved to become its own health insurance provider. It opened its own medical clinic and heavily subsidized preventive care for its teachers and staff. This has kept health care cost growth at 4–5% a year and allowed the district to absorb the costs without passing them onto educators.

The local community has rewarded this fiscal stewardship with two major wins in elections. In 2012, over 70% of voters supported a $1.2 billion bond measure to modernize buildings. Carvalho promised that all the work would be done by the private sector and that these dollars would not add to the district's bureaucracy. He kept his word. As a result, 72% of voters in November 2018 approved a referendum for more funding for teacher pay, which, according to Carvalho, will increase salaries in the district by 13 to 23%. Zero dollars will go toward administration.

Lessons

The first lesson from Miami is that hard financial times offer an opportunity to rethink how things are done. Many districts need to rework vendor contracts, health care arrangements, pensions, and a host of other costly facets of their operation. When times are good, administrators can look stingy trying to rework these agreements. When times are tough, the opportunity is there.

This is not to say that districts shouldn't try to rework contracts and such in better financial times. As it turns out, reworking long-term obligations can keep good times going and also blunt the effects of bad times. It is simply to say that it is easier when times are tough, and savvy administrators should realize that and leverage it.

Second, Miami teaches us that communities respect and will reward fiscal responsibility, even though doing the right thing can be difficult. Renegotiating agreements can breed discontent—as, certainly, can firing staff. Over the long term, however, prudent financial management can yield more resources. Citizens are skeptical of big building projects, realizing that they can be venues for waste, fraud, and abuse. Miami-Dade was wise to take this head-on and made promises to the community that it would do everything possible to try to prevent that. When they succeeded, it made going back to the voters for higher teacher pay easier. Yet even with that, the district again promised that the money would go where it was supposed to and not bloat the administration of the district.

If districts want more money, the best thing they can do is prove to their constituents that they will spend it well.

Third, Miami shows that the staffing surge is not inevitable; districts don't have to do it, and they will be okay if they don't. When asked about stemming the rising tide of administrative staff, Carvalho himself says, "It was not a function of destiny or happenstance." The district made deliberate choices in the budgeting process to change that. Any district that wants to could do the same.

ACADEMIES OF MATH AND SCIENCE CHARTER SCHOOLS: STRETCHING THE SCHOOL CONSTRUCTION DOLLAR

The Academies of Math and Science (AMS) Charter Schools operate seven schools educating more than 3,900 students in Arizona. Founded in 2000 by Tatyana Chayka, an immigrant from Uzbekistan who came to the United States following the collapse of the Soviet Union, and Sergey Shayevich, the network prides itself on locating its schools only in underserved areas and serving students who have not found other schools that meet their needs. One of the first students of AMS was Ms. Chayka's son Kim, who today serves as co-CEO with her.

In Arizona, charter schools receive, on average, $8,523 in total funding per student ("Overview of K–12 Per Pupil Funding," 2019). This is $951 less than traditional public schools, which have access to transportation and capital funding that charter schools do not. As charters seek to expand to meet demand and needs, the lack of facilities (or the wherewithal to build new ones) puts a serious damper on growth.

AMS charter schools want to grow. In the 2020–2021 school year, for example, AMS (n.d.) is opening nine more schools that will serve 8,000 students. Demand is growing in part due to AMS's strong performance. Its flagship campus was recognized as a National Blue Ribbon school in 2008 and Arizona Charter of the Year in 2016. It consistently has received an "A" rating from Arizona's accountability system. The Math and Science Success Academy in South Tucson also was given an "A" rating by the state in 2018.

To grow, AMS must figure out how to finance the construction of new schools in a financially manageable way. Too much debt would hamper its ability to sustain the STEAM-centered, small-class-size education that is central to the AMS model. It cannot drown in debt payments.

Steven Hykes, CFO of AMS, highlights three areas where AMS has been able to stretch the school construction dollar: site placement, credit enhancement, and cost control.[3] Each is worth discussing.

Deciding where to open a school is fraught with issues. Are there enough nearby students who will want to attend it? Are there other schools close at hand? Is real estate affordable? These are some key questions that AMS works through when deciding where to locate a school.

First, AMS estimates demand. It creates a multivariate statistical model, fed with data from real estate research firms, to estimate how many children live in the area being considered. It looks at the average performance of traditional public schools in the area and potential competition from nearby charters. This creates a kind of "heat map" for potential demand. To reach the economies of scale AMS seeks, it prefers to serve around 1,000 students in a school.

Second, AMS looks at the competition. The number of nearby charters is part of the model, and AMS tries to gauge how much competitive pressure it might have as it tries to reach the optimal number of students. Hykes cautions that conditions can change quickly, as Arizona authorizes new charters every year. Since AMS takes a 2-year planning cycle to identify neighborhoods and open schools, much can capsize its forecasts.

Third, AMS looks at real estate prices. As Hykes explained, a swing of even $500,000 in real estate costs becomes a huge difference in the long term.

Ultimately, AMS tries to triangulate demand, competition, and real estate cost. If it can get enough of the first without too much of the second and third, AMS will try to open a school there. But any one of those three can kill the deal.

Once AMS settles on a site, it needs to finance the school. Like many other charter schools around the country, it issues bonds to finance the debt. These bonds are then paid off over a long window (up to 30 or 35 years).

Debt is expensive for charter schools. As Hykes explained, "Most schools value liquidity over interest rate." They need the money now and rarely have substantial capital for a down payment or collateral, so they have to pay higher interest rates to reflect their riskier debt. Over long periods, even a 1–2% difference in interest rates can mean huge amounts of money.

AMS has been able to take advantage of a new program from the state that backed its debt and lowered its interest rate. The Arizona Public School Credit Enhancement Program created a $100 million pot of money that acts as a guarantee for school borrowing, lowering the risk of lending to schools and thus their interest rates. Both district and charter schools may take advantage of this fund. Schools that would like to do so apply to a state Credit Enhancement Eligibility Board, which decides which schools are approved and for how much enhancement (RBC Capital Markets, 2016).

The upshot? For the $23.4 million in enhanced debt AMS secured, it saved roughly $1 million. That is $1 million that can be plowed back into the schools.

And of course, once AMS has identified a location and secured financing, it actually has to build the school. As anyone who has watched a home improvement show on television has seen, costs can spiral quickly. AMS has worked to control the variables present in any project to keep construction costs reasonable.

First, it works with architects and developers to "value engineer" the project. Kim Chayka, co-CEO of AMS, goes so far as to look at futures markets for key construction components like timber to try to get the best value from the construction materials. As lumber prices rose, AMS transitioned to building with concrete blocks. Most buildings in Arizona are built with a "stick frame" of wood, but not AMS's new schools. Concrete was substantially less expensive. It also works to create positive aesthetic design features that don't cost much extra money, like outdoor hallways and open spaces that take advantage of Arizona's climate. AMS is quite purposeful about the features it designs and includes to make sure to keep prices down.

Then AMS works with the general contractors and subcontractors to negotiate good rates on the front end. Experienced project managers know that once construction starts, contractors have leverage and can try to renegotiate when clients are vulnerable. AMS makes sure to avoid these situations by getting everything hammered out up front.

Third, AMS tries to work with municipalities to control costs. Municipalities can be of great help or hindrance during construction projects. Each has its own peculiarities with permits, inspections, and other requests (like fixing roads that lead to projects or electrical infrastructure that feeds projects). AMS tries to be proactive in its relationship with municipalities to make sure that unexpected costs and delays don't emerge mid-project, but it also is mindful about where it locates its schools. If a municipality has a habit of making construction difficult, AMS will be less likely to locate there, even if other parts of the decision matrix point to that location.

AMS has a couple of other things going for it as well. Builders can build nearly year-round in Arizona, given its dry climate. The cost of living and rates of unionization are lower as well.

Still, schools across Arizona have these same climate and labor conditions but are not as efficient as AMS. As Matthew Ladner of the Arizona Chamber of Commerce, who's also the author of Chapter 1 of this volume, has argued, Arizona districts are not stretching their school construction dollars (Ladner, 2019). Their facilities spending has risen even as enrollment has declined. Ladner estimates that Arizona contains more than 1.4 million square feet of vacant or underutilized school space, yet districts are continuing to build, seemingly oblivious to future projections of student enrollment. It's not too surprising that Arizona's district teachers have salary grievances.

Why is this happening? Ladner's explanation is politics. Architecture firms and construction companies have much to gain from building big new schools and thus donate substantially to school board races and bond referenda. Politicians like to build things, so everybody wins—other than teachers and students.

This helps us understand why other schools and school districts don't approach the economics of construction in the same way the Academies of Math and Science Charter Schools do. Given the varied circumstances of schools across the state, as well as the country writ large, there is likely no one answer, but a reasonable hypothesis is the twin *lack of capacity* and *politics*. Negotiating building contracts and value engineering buildings are not covered during traditional school administrator preparation. Maybe a district, or a charter school, would be lucky to have a school board member with experience in construction, but those are not required qualities for overseeing one of these institutions. Plus, there's little incentive to do better. Powerful interests in the community want to see big expensive school buildings, and bucking those interests comes at a cost that may thwart even the most knowledgeable policymaker.

Lessons

AMS can teach charter, district, and private school leaders a number of important lessons. Want money to hire great teachers? You need to control costs elsewhere. Want a nice and enticing building? You need to understand construction costs and the trade-offs necessary to make that happen.

AMS's first lesson is that leaders must sweat the small and noninstructional stuff. It's no fun to track the price differential between timber and prefabricated concrete blocks, but deciding between them can have a huge impact on a school's financial prospects. Understanding the implications of even small differences in interest rates for long-term debt can mean hundreds of thousands of dollars in budget impact years down the road. Similarly, taking a hard look at where to locate schools and studiously analyzing the potential market and the competition are things that schools have to do, and do thoughtfully.

Particularly in places where schooling is getting more competitive, such prosaic details make the difference. It simply won't be enough to operate a better-than-average school. Competition for teaching talent will increase, and schools will need to figure out how to offer more attractive salary and benefit packages. Families will expect more, and more diverse, offerings, from extra-curriculars to robotics. To afford these programs, schools will need to know how to find savings in areas like construction and debt servicing.

The second important lesson is for state leaders who want to see more high-quality schools. Arizona has been able to support school growth without spending any money. By simply setting dollars that the state possesses aside in a credit-enhancing fund, the state has enabled schools to borrow money at much lower interest rates. Yes, that set-aside money can't simply be moved somewhere else in the budget to fund some other state priority. It is also true that there is risk associated with those dollars, and a major default could take a big chunk out of it. But, with careful consideration of who should have the money lent to them, that risk is low, and over time that money should grow with its own investments.

Other states could look into creating such funds. Some, like Colorado, Texas, and Utah, have similar programs, but many more could do the same. Rather than getting themselves on the hook for the entirety of a school construction project, they could provide targeted credit enhancement to help schools and districts finance the projects themselves. The cost and risk are then spread across several different institutions.

Third, administrator preparation programs and organizations that support and train charter and traditional school boards should make facilities financing and construction supervision part of their programs. State school board associations could create training modules on building efficiently, as could state charter school organizations. But principals need to know this as well, so taking time in preparation programs to focus explicitly on school construction costs and the sources of financing that schools can utilize would be time well spent.

Finally, the leaders of teacher and administrator unions should understand the trade-offs between school construction spending and professionals' salaries and benefits. Even when construction funding comes from separate budget and revenue lines, construction isn't the only expense associated with school buildings; when a building is overbuilt or uses inefficient materials, upkeep eats into the money pots that pay for salaries and benefits.

SETON EDUCATION PARTNERS:
LEVERAGING TECHNOLOGY IN CASH-STRAPPED SCHOOLS

"We will reduce their per-pupil operating costs." So promises Emily Gilbride, director of the Seton Blended Learning Network, a program within the non-profit organization Seton Education Partners.[4] Seton teams up with Catholic schools to promote blended learning to increase enrollment at a faster pace than costs and thereby help return the schools to a financially stable footing.

The financial plight of Catholic schools in America is a familiar tale. Since their peak in the 1960s, they've seen declining enrollment and rising costs, leading to the shuttering of many schools. As Andy Smarick and Kelly Robson wrote in 2015, "While in 1965 more than 13,000 Catholic schools served 5.6 million students, 50 years later there were 6,568 schools serving 1.9 million students" (p. 11).

While the general secularization of society and increased tolerance for Catholics in public schools are part of the story, the main driver of Catholic schools' present plight has been their human capital model. Historically, Catholic schools relied upon members of religious vocations like priests and sisters to teach students. They had the gravitas, the support of parents to teach large classes, and the religious commitment to take very low salaries. As religious vocations declined, Catholic schools had to turn more and more to lay teachers and administrators, both increasing costs and decreasing class sizes.

Small class sizes are now a feature of many Catholic schools across the country and a selling point for parents. The problem, of course, is that the smaller the class size, the higher the per-pupil expense, even when staff salaries are generally well below those of most public schools. Particularly for schools that want to serve low-income populations, and even for schools that want to serve middle-class families, this makes the financial model problematic, if not untenable.

Seton Education Partners is working with 14 Catholic schools around the country to change the equation. In the schools where Seton works, it encourages classrooms to grow, often from an average of 15 to 30 students per class. To cope with these additional students, classes are divided into two or three smaller instructional units that progress through the day in what Gilbride calls a "rotational small-group model." While one group is working with the teacher, the others are on Chromebooks, working with computer-adaptive software like i-Read, Imagine Math, and Lexia Learning. In all, Seton leverages 14 different software platforms, depending on the school, grade, and student need.

Because only half of the class, at most, is on computers at a time, Seton partner schools need only a two-to-one ratio of children to Chromebooks, instead of the more costly and intensive one-to-one programs that many schools use. This model also requires little change to the physical structures of schools and of classrooms. Usually Seton just adds some tables along one classroom wall to serve as computer stations, plus some kidney-shaped tables for small-group work with teachers.

St. Joseph Catholic School in Cincinnati, OH, was able to grow from 202 to 282 students in its initial year of partnership. As most of those children participate in Ohio's EdChoice school voucher program, each additional pupil represented $4,650 in new revenue for the school. All told, that meant almost $400,000 more coming into the school on an annual basis.

The most recent addition to the Seton portfolio, the Immaculate Conception School in Dayton, OH, was able to increase its enrollment by 90 students in its first year of partnership. Again, this means hundreds of thousands more dollars in revenue every year. For small Catholic schools, this is a massive swing in enrollment and revenue and a massive opportunity to serve more students.

Moving to larger classes and blended learning hasn't been easy, however. Both parents and teachers need convincing—and teachers need training and technical help. With respect to parents, Gilbride argues that focusing on the personalization that is possible through computer-adaptive software is a big selling point. Also, schools don't double their classrooms overnight. Usually they add a few children per year, which cushions the shock, allowing parents to ease into the new model. The story for teachers is similar. By easing into the model, providing instructional coaches (Seton places coaches in schools for the first 2 years of a partnership), and focusing on the upside for teachers, Seton can win them over. It also helps them keep their jobs in the face of their school potentially closing.

"We want to place each child's God-given potential at the forefront of what we're doing," Gilbride says, which helps focus both families and teachers on what is important.

Seton's partnership is a multiyear agreement with schools to help get their blended-learning program up and running and support them as they transition to operating it independently. Seton fundraises for the startup costs of the transition, which can range from $600,000 for a small school to $850,000 for a larger one. This money goes toward purchasing hardware and software, upgrading servers and wiring, and hiring an instructional coach for teachers. After that, schools pay a fee to the network to continue to participate. Note, though, that Seton's bulk purchasing of software licenses, which are then made available to network schools, saves participating schools more than they pay in their network fee. Software licenses are expensive.

It is important to note, though, that for the Seton model to work, several stars need to align. There must be leadership in the school willing to do something different. There must be someone who understands the financial situation and the need to increase revenue at a faster rate than expenses. There must be teachers willing to buy in. Parents need to buy in. It is not simply blended learning, but a school culture that wants to do something different to balance the budget and educate children. Not every school has this kind of leadership or this kind of community.

Lessons

Blended learning is not for everyone, but Gilbride offers two lessons for schools considering a move in that direction, lessons that easily apply to private and public schools alike.

First, schools looking to try blended learning need not plan for one-to-one student-to-device ratios. One-to-one is a phenomenon that has swept the nation, and schools have been purchasing huge numbers of tablets and Chromebooks to meet the demand. These devices require updates to servers and routers and sometimes even to electrical wiring in schools. They must be maintained, they require tech support, and the more of these devices, the higher those costs are. Yes, if class sizes are increasing or other changes are being made, the thought that children are getting their very own computers or tablets can help blunt criticism. But blunting criticism in the short term is arguably not worth the trade-off in the long term.

Gilbride argues that a two-to-one ratio is better. Her primary argument is that it "allows teachers to teach." Rather than having students constantly glued to devices, there are times when students use devices and there are times when they don't. There's time for traditional instruction or small-group work and time to work with the adaptive software. It allows each of those elements—teachers and software—to do what it does best.

Two-to-one is also undeniably cheaper. Buying, supporting, and maintaining half the devices of a one-to-one program can represent serious cost savings. For schools with very narrow margins in their budgets, this can be a game-changer. There are still substantial startup costs, though. It should not be overlooked that Seton needs to do fundraising on the front end to make the transition.

Second, Gilbride encourages schools to start small. Transitioning to a blended model is a huge shift for students, teachers, leaders, and parents. It is not something that should be done lightly or quickly. It can go very wrong.

The software itself need not cost much. Numerous free, high-quality software programs have many of the features of the software that Seton and other blended-learning providers use. They are not as fully articulated as the paid programs, but they can give schools a rough idea of the types of things that teachers and students will be able to do if they switch to a blended model. Examples include ISL, No Red Ink, and, perhaps most famously, the Khan Academy.

Schools can pilot blended learning with these free tools in one classroom or grade to see how the model works. Rather than immediately trying to scale up to the entire school, teachers and principals can dip their toes in the water and see what the temperature is. Do teachers like the model? Are children responding to it? What are the practical concerns (i.e., what infrastructure upgrading will need to take place, how might schedules need to change, etc.)? In short, is this something worth trying on a larger scale? Only after success with the pilot program will schools need to make the large investments in equipment and training to move to an entirely blended model.

These lessons apply beyond blended learning. Any decision to use technology should focus on what problem that technology is trying to solve. If it is iPads or SMART boards or Chromebooks or whatever the technology of tomorrow will be, starting with small pilot programs is a wise first step. Also, thinking about how students can share resources, instead of requiring one device for every child, can be a way to save costs.

CONCLUSION

Why should school districts care about slowing the growth of nonteaching staff? Well, if they want to be able to pay teachers more, offer smaller classes, improve facilities, or reduce the kinds of compliance and box-checking that large bureaucracies create, trimming the nonteaching staff can help accomplish these goals.

Why should teachers or parents care about the time and energy that school leaders invest in school construction? Shouldn't school leaders be focused on instruction? Well, if they want to pay teachers more, offer more diverse courses and programs, be able to construct buildings that students and teachers want to go to every day, or be able to locate in areas of high demand and draw in students and the funding that comes with them, saving money on capital expenses can help accomplish those goals.

Why should parents get on board with blended learning? Well, if they're in a school on the verge of closure or want to provide more depth or breadth in academic offerings, blended learning can help change both the economics of the school and the education that it provides. Blended learning is not just for schools facing financial difficulty. It can, for another example, assist rural schools that cannot recruit teachers for higher level math and science courses that provide challenging coursework for more advanced students.

In all cases, stretching the school dollar is not the end in itself; it is simply the means to providing a great education to children who need and want it. The three school networks profiled here illustrate ways that schools can do just that.

NOTES

1. Email correspondence with Dr. Ben Scafidi, April 2019.
2. Interview with Alberto Carvalho, April 26, 2019.
3. Interview with Steven Hykes, April 10, 2019.
4. Interview with Emily Gilbride, April 24, 2019.

REFERENCES

Academies of Math and Science. (n.d.). *Nearly two decades of proven results.* amscharters.org/our-story/

Florida Department of Education. (2019). *Educational Funding Accountability Act: Summary of administrative expenditures.* www.fldoe.org/finance/fl-edu-finance -program-fefp/edual-funding-accountability-act-summa.stml

Ladner, M. (2019, July 8). *Column: Born in Arizona, moved to Babylonia, got surplus school space made of stona.* Chamber Business News. chamberbusinessnews .com/2019/07/08/column-born-in-arizona-moved-to-babylonia-got-surplus -school-space-made-of-stona

Overview of K–12 per pupil funding for school districts and charter schools. (2019, June 17). www.azleg.gov/jlbc/districtvscharterfunding.pdf

Payscale.com. (2019). *Cost of living calculator.* www.payscale.com/cost-of-living -calculator/Florida-Miami/New-York-New-York

RBC Capital Markets. (2016, November). *Arizona public school credit enhancement program: Program and funding overview.* education.azgovernor.gov/sites /default/files/presentation_on_financing_structure_-_rbc_capital_markets.pdf

Scafidi, B. (2017, May). *Back to the staffing surge.* EdChoice. www.edchoice.org /wp-content/uploads/2017/05/Back-to-the-Staffing-Surge-by-Ben-Scafidi.pdf

Smarick, A., & Robson, K. (2015). *Catholic school renaissance: A wise giver's guide to strengthening a national asset.* The Philanthropy Roundtable.

U.S. Census Bureau. (2016). *2016 public elementary–secondary education finance data.* www.census.gov/data/tables/2016/econ/school-finances/secondary -education-finance.html

CHAPTER 5

How the "Would You Rather" Test Can Help With School Finance Decisions

Marguerite Roza

On average, U.S. school districts now spend about $14,000 per student per year (National Education Association, 2019). Many in education are struggling with how to balance increased demands on schools amid rising costs. Because schooling resources are inherently constrained, it's incumbent on leaders to consider the costs and benefits of all available options (Chingos & Whitehurst, 2011). Using a "would you rather" test can help.

The classic "would you rather" party game poses two or more equally appealing (or unappealing) hypothetical scenarios and asks players to choose one. It's a common pastime for kids and an icebreaker for adults. Would you rather eat a cup of worms or go a month without bathing? Would you rather have lunch with Prince Harry or Justin Bieber? And so on.

I suggest we use the "would you rather" exercise to explore trade-offs in school spending and think through the value of various cost-equivalent investments. For example, one survey asked teachers whether they preferred (a) a reduction in class size by two students, (b) the addition of aide support for 20% of the time, or (c) $5,000 cash via pay raise. (More on the results of this survey later.) The "would you rather" choices can include options for how a portion of public education funds might be spent. Parents, teachers, and other stakeholders would be invited to weigh their preferences among different cost-equivalent scenarios. Where one option is simply to receive the cash in lieu of a program or service, those weighing alternatives have a clear view of the cost of the options before them.

The time is especially ripe for more "would you rather" explorations of costs and value, in large part because of a groundbreaking new federal requirement for financial transparency at the level of the individual school. Education leaders nationwide now have access to a treasure trove of per-pupil, school-specific spending data for every school in the country. These data should make calculating cost-equivalent options much more feasible—and almost certainly will give rise to thorny spending debates in many communities. Add to that the financial strain from an economic downturn and escalating teacher pension debt and health care costs. These pressures come amid recent proposals to expand publicly funded schooling—from universal pre-K to free college. Substantial new investments deserve responsible vetting and add urgency to the need for new finance solutions with finite (and possibly shrinking) dollars. And finally, messaging research tells us that the public trusts leaders who talk in terms of cost-equivalent trade-offs and dollars linked to students—and most governmental (and, for that matter, private) systems could stand to build more trust right now.

EDUCATION SPENDING ALWAYS INVOLVES CHOICES: SMART CHOICES REQUIRE UNDERSTANDING VALUE FOR THE DOLLAR

Any time we spend public funds on one thing, we've essentially chosen not to spend that money on something else. These choices should be made on the basis of careful consideration. At the core, "would you rather" offers an exploratory but often missed step that forces us to reflect on our assumptions about how a program or service is best structured, for what outcomes, and at what cost. The test is a tool to help us to press pause on our inertia-infused thinking around schooling and to expose perspectives that can both help students and wrestle with increasing demands amid cost constraints.

This is not a novel idea. In 2011, for example, Goldhaber et al. surveyed Washington State teachers with the "would you rather" question cited above, seeking their preferences among cost-equivalent investments in smaller classes, more aides, or salary increases.

Importantly, each option by itself would have roughly the same cost implications for the district. The results showed that an overwhelming majority of teachers (more than 80%) preferred the pay hike. This was surprising given that other survey research had suggested that teachers preferred smaller classes and improved working conditions over higher salary.

The problem with much of the previous research on these kinds of trade-offs is that it didn't ask teachers to wrestle with cost-equivalent options (e.g., Teoh & Coggins, 2012). In fact, most previous work exploring preferences on teacher compensation and

> **TEACHERS:**
> **WOULD YOU RATHER HAVE**
>
> a. two fewer students in class;
> b. an aide for 20% of the time; or
> c. a $5,000/year raise?

working conditions included no hard numbers at all, leaving it up to the teacher to imagine what magnitude of raise they might get when deciding what would influence a decision to stay in teaching—higher salary or better working conditions (e.g., Futernick, 2007). But the numbers matter. Whether the potential raise is $1,000, $5,000, or $20,000 is essential to the decision. Similarly, knowing whether class sizes drop by two students, five students, or more matters, too. That's where it becomes important to clarify cost-equivalent scenarios to see which strategy offers more value for the stakeholder at a given cost.

It's clear that the dollar amount matters. Consider another example: Imagine asking parents of qualified preschoolers if they'd rather (a) send their child to a publicly funded full-day preschool or (b) get a check for the roughly $12,000 that it typically costs to deliver that service. What if the publicly provided preschool cost upwards of $30,000 per pupil, as it does in Seattle (Parsons, 2018)? If the "would you rather" trade-off above was offered, some rightly would point out that $30,000 is more than twice the stated market rate of $12,000. The $30,000 city-subsidized preschool might be higher-quality than a $12,000 market-rate preschool, but is it $18,000 better? If the city instead gave parents the $30,000 in cash, some parents might be able to have more time at home, perhaps taking advantage of a low-cost co-op preschool, or use the funds to raise the family's income level out of poverty. Some will ask what's driving the higher costs of the program in their particular city—and in the process perhaps uncover more productive options for the city's limited resources.

In the lead-up to a 2018 ballot measure asking voters to fund the preschool program, Seattle's estimated per-pupil figures remained a mystery. City leaders had not publicly shared any per-pupil expenses in their plans. As the initiative went to ballot, Shelby Parsons, a University of Washington graduate student, dug into city documents to compute expenses of some $30,000 per pupil. After doing this analysis, Parsons (2018) suggested a trade-off: Eliminate some program bells and whistles to reduce per-pupil cost to $15,000 (still above market rate) and use the savings to expand the reach of publicly funded preschool to all the city's 3- and 4-year-olds from low-income households. Perhaps if Seattle leaders had paused to do a "would you rather" test, they could have surfaced still other options that better leveraged public dollars to meet the desired societal outcomes: making quality preschool widely available and affordable.

At first blush, the "would you rather" test may come across as glib or even irresponsible, particularly where policy leaders worry that stakeholders may make purely self-interested decisions. What if parents don't spend the money on their children? And shouldn't it be up to system leaders to decide what's best for students anyway? On the flip

> **PARENTS:**
> **WOULD YOU RATHER**
>
> a. enroll your 4-year-old child in a publicly funded preschool, or
> b. receive a check for $12,000? What if the check was for $30,000?

side, one could argue that parents also have their child's best interest in mind. And giving lower-income families the cash in lieu of the service may be a better way to mitigate poverty's effects.

This back-and-forth about what's the best use of public funding for the beneficiary is precisely what makes the discussion worthwhile. The "would you rather" exercise offers needed perspective on resource decisions and serves as a mechanism to reestablish the connection between money and the value of the program or service provided. The goal of the exercise is to inform financial decisions so that they may be modified or strengthened to get maximum value for the dollar.

The concept works for smaller-ticket spending items, too. One Pacific Northwest school recently used the "would you rather" approach in deciding among options, which would be costequivalent to the school, for the girls' lacrosse program.[1] The school had a combined team with another school, but many players wanted their own school team. A cost analysis indicated that severing the joint arrangement to create two teams would increase annual expenditures by about $200 per player. Parents and players were asked whether they preferred the existing joint arrangement at no cost to the players or the separate team arrangement that carried a $200 per-player fee. Ultimately, while players preferred separate teams, they decided it wasn't worth the $200 if they had to pay it themselves.

School leaders used "would you rather" to gauge the value of separate teams to those requesting that the school create them. By surfacing and sharing the per-player cost, all could attach an incremental price to the effort, and all (including those advocating for the change) could assess whether the positive value was actually worth the

> **PARENTS AND PLAYERS OF HIGH SCHOOL LACROSSE:**
> **WOULD YOU RATHER**
>
> a. play on a combined team with a nearby school at no extra cost, or
> b. establish a separate team but pay a $200 fee per player?

cost. School leaders could then incorporate this valuable information alongside other factors (e.g., ensuring equity across athletic offerings) in making their final decisions.

IS GIVING OUT CASH A REASONABLE OPTION?

On a practical level, offering cash as an alternative to a program or service isn't always appropriate as a real-world alternative. And while individuals may be interested in the cash, those individual interests must be weighed against the societal interest in a given policy approach. When it comes to public funds and applying the "would you rather" test, public interest ordinarily should trump purely private interests. That said, there may be scenarios where the cash may make more sense in achieving the desired societal outcomes in a financially sustainable way.

To be clear, offering cash isn't some hypothetical concept. In philanthropy, efforts are already underway to alleviate poverty by giving people money instead of delivering programs or supplies, with some of the world's foremost researchers of antipoverty strategies engaged in an independent study of the emerging data (Aizenman, 2017). The GiveDirectly philanthropy (www .givedirectly.org), founded by four graduate economics students, is based on the idea that giving cash with no strings attached yields a greater benefit for those experiencing extreme poverty than the traditional approach of offering aid via services. The philanthropy's premise is that decisions about what recipients need are best made by the recipients themselves.

In education, leaders seem far more inclined to respond to problems by designing new programs or services than by giving out cash. For instance, common proposals to address teacher shortages in specific areas (such as math and science or in high-poverty schools) include new teacher residency programs, programs to better support and prepare teachers, improved HR practices, loan forgiveness programs, and so on (Podolsky et al., 2016). But research suggests that direct bonuses to teachers in shortage areas are the most cost-effective option to improve retention (Bueno & Sass, 2018). Yet leaders continue to avoid the cash option. Chad Aldeman (2019) says as much in his reaction to the California governor's recent proposal: "Instead of a convoluted loan forgiveness program, California should just send the money directly to teachers."

But what about students? Could we legitimately consider options that give cash *to students or their families*? The idea here is different from voucher or education savings account initiatives, which tend to be constructed by a separate authority to let public dollars flow outside the public system to a private entity. What we're considering is whether those *inside* the public system would consider an allocation of their funds directly to beneficiaries of their services as part of their delivery model.

Roland Fryer (2010) studied what happens when districts offer direct cash incentives to students to work harder in school. He found that the cash incentives are effective at raising performance when designed around student efforts (versus outcomes). More important, he found that such cash payments yielded student achievement increases comparable to those linked to success-

> **PARENTS OF KINDERGARTNERS:**
> **WOULD YOU RATHER THE SCHOOL DISTRICT**
>
> a. deposit $50 in a college savings account for your child, or
> b. use the $50 to augment spending on services for kindergartners?

ful reforms of recent decades—*but at lower cost* (and without decreases in intrinsic motivation). Despite the cost-effective results, however, very few districts use direct cash incentives to students as part of a broader resource allocation strategy, suggesting an overall reluctance to give cash to students and families.

One of the few existing family cash incentive examples is San Francisco's Kindergarten 2 College program, Save for College (sfgov.org/ofe/k2c), which aims to boost college attendance by simply giving students money. Each child entering the San Francisco Unified School District automatically gets a $50 college savings account. Unlike our philanthropy example, here the cash has strings attached: Families can't withdraw money until the child graduates from high school, and the money can be spent only on postsecondary educational expenses. To be sure, the current allocation is a tiny sum, amounting to less than half of 1% of the roughly $13,000 the district spends per pupil, although California's Governor Newsom did propose in his 2019–2020 budget using state dollars to expand such programs. While the sum is small, the program's goal isn't to fully fund higher education, but rather to increase parental expectations for their child's education, which district leaders hope will impact college-going.

Most of the time, the direct-cash approach isn't considered, even when it seems like a potential win-win. A recent story describes how the School District of Philadelphia spends nearly $60,000 per pupil to transport some students with disabilities to and from school in taxis with an aide (Wolfman-Arent, 2018). Even at this price, transportation is unreliable and parents are frustrated. Might a better option be to offer parents the cash in return for getting their own children to school? At a $60,000 price tag for some children, those parents might choose to modify their working hours or quit their job altogether. Instead, the district appears increasingly reliant on the costly program, doubling to more than 400 the number of taxis transporting between one and four students to school in 2018. Where districts reimburse families for transportation, they tend to do it at much lower cost than the cost to the district of transporting those same students (Nebraska Department of Education, 2017).

Whether one seriously considers the cash option or not, taking the time to pencil out a range of cost-equivalent options, where one option is a cash transfer, serves to attach a dollar value to the discussion. This action alone can help clarify whether the status quo arrangement is delivering in a cost-effective fashion a program or service that is valued by those it serves—and reaping the desired outcomes. If options are presented, and teachers, parents, or students say they'd rather have the cash, that can be a strong signal that something in the current delivery model may not be right. Perhaps the service being provided has become too costly or isn't delivering the intended value. Either way, it signals that the time has come to creatively brainstorm options.

FOLLOW FOUR STEPS TO USE THE "WOULD YOU RATHER" TEST

Here's how financial strategy works in most districts and states: When revenues are growing, leaders identify a desired strategy or investment and then explore whether they can muster the needed funding. The goal might be to lower class sizes, increase student supports, or expand elective offerings.

Financial experts then compute the incremental costs of the effort (say, $19 million to put a social worker in every school). When times are tight and budgets must be cut, the process works in reverse. A district might reduce librarians for an incremental savings of $12 million, and so on.

But these approaches miss a critical part of the process: considering various cost-equivalent trade-offs in terms of the *per-unit* costs and value *to the beneficiary* (e.g., students, families, teachers, or schools). The following four steps can help ensure that a more complete range of options gets considered.

Step #1: Put Spending in Per-Unit Costs

The way education figures traditionally are compiled and discussed—arranged by "function" or "object" categories like "instruction" or salaries, benefits, or debt service—makes it too easy to miss the forest for the trees. Converting money into per-unit terms helps put the focus squarely back on the forest. "Per student" is typically the default unit used. But the unit also can be per teacher or per school, and the like, depending on what is to be compared.

The process essentially involves breaking down bigger numbers into per-pupil terms using simple division. The denominator is the relevant student group—most commonly those who participate in the program or service. For instance, in the Philadelphia transportation example above, the district spent

> **PARENTS:**
> **WOULD YOU RATHER**
>
> a. have lower class sizes for all 12 years of schooling, or
> b. receive the nearly $1,800 per year investment (over $20,000 total) in cash?

$38 million on the taxi service and aides involved in transporting the identified special education students. Dividing $38 million by the number of students riding solo in taxis gives the cost per student transported, roughly $60,000 per individual pupil.

Often, the larger the expenditure, the less likely it is that leaders will break it down into per-unit costs. But that's precisely when it is important to compare spending on a relative basis. Take the 2016 Washington State I-1351 ballot initiative for class-size reduction, which was estimated to cost $1.7 billion per year at full implementation. Class-size reduction is generally popular, but what was missing from the big number was the per-unit piece. Dividing the total cost by the number of public school pupils in the state showed that the effort would raise spending by nearly $1,800 per student, per year—or well over $20,000 over 12 years of schooling. While the $1.7 billion figure didn't get much of a reaction, many of the graduate students in my University of Washington finance course reacted with urgency to the per-student one. They weren't sure that the state's students would realize $20,000 worth of value from the change.

Without comparable costs, leaders can get distracted by false equivalence. I've heard proposals to fund more teacher planning time with the savings realized from reduced reliance on textbooks. The problem is that such investments in teacher planning time tend to cost more than four times the per-pupil amount realized from reducing textbooks (based on author calculations). A $425,000 donation from Acuity Insurance for the naming rights on the Grafton High School gym seemed like an outsized advantage among Wisconsin districts (Johnson, 2019). Putting the figure in per-pupil terms by dividing the sum across the number of students over the length of the relationship clarifies that the resources amount to $24 per high school pupil (in a district spending more than $12,000 per pupil in public funds). While at first blush $425,000 seems like a big number, $24 per pupil seems less relevant.

The cost of sick days is an instance where exploring per-*teacher*, versus per-student, costs makes sense. Typically, teachers earn and take sick days without knowing the cost implications for the district. In fact, the costs of substitutes range from about $90–$200 per teacher, per day. Armed with the per-unit costs,

> **TEACHERS:**
> **WOULD YOU RATHER**
>
> a. keep all your sick days for possible future need, or
> b. trade any unused sick days for $100/per day?
> What if it was $200/per day?

some schools have surfaced creative alternatives—such as providing cash incentives (of, say, $100 per unused day) to reduce teacher absenteeism (and, ultimately, reduce costly end-of-career payouts plaguing some districts associated with unused sick days) (Bock, 2011).

Converting dollars into per-pupil or per-teacher terms better conveys the relative magnitude of spending, identifies out-of-whack spending, and helps surface spending trade-offs.

Step #2: Construct Cost-Equivalent Trade-Offs: Co-Production Can Help

If the first step is to put spending into per-unit costs, the second step is to construct cost-equivalent trade-offs, including potentially offering the cash to the intended beneficiary. Often, of course, the most challenging part is coming up with plausible alternatives.

In our Certificate in Education Finance program at Georgetown (n.d.), we have participants compute a range of cost-equivalent options from the perspective of the school. We ask whether their school would rather have a vice principal or offer $5,000 stipends for

> **PRINCIPALS:**
> **WOULD YOU RATHER HAVE**
>
> a. a vice principal, or
> b. enough money to award 24 teachers a stipend of $5,000 for extra duties of your choosing?

24 of the school's existing teachers. We ask whether their school would be better off with one full-time reading coach or a summer reading program

serving 120 students. And during a budget cut, whether they'd prefer to eliminate a librarian or raise class sizes in music and PE to 35. And so on. Importantly, participants have done the math to ensure that the proffered options are indeed cost-neutral.

Another trade-off explores the annual cost of living allowance, or COLA—a common fixture in schooling whereby teachers get a fixed percentage increase (say, 4%) for each step that they rise on the salary schedule. Converting the percentage raise to a dollar figure across all teachers reveals that it amounts to an average of $2,400 per teacher (assuming an average teacher salary of $60,000). But if, as in most districts, attrition is highest among junior teachers, the fixed percentage may have limited benefit in diminishing turnover where it's highest. For each junior teacher making $40,000 a year, the fixed-percentage raise will yield only $1,600, versus $3,200 per senior teacher making $80,000 a year. A cost-equivalent alternative would be to instead award a fixed *dollar* amount to all teachers (e.g., $2,400), which uses the same limited pot of money to deliver more to the teachers most likely to leave (Roza, 2015). Denver did just this in 2017, when it awarded a flat $1,400 per teacher (Denver Public Schools, 2017).

Regardless of whether the financial change involves a new investment or a budget cut, education leaders typically default to a relatively narrow band of options, which tends to boil down to the hiring of new staff or the elimination of existing staff. An emerging concept

> **JUNIOR TEACHERS:**
> **WOULD YOU RATHER HAVE**
>
> a. a 4% pay raise per teacher, or
> b. a fixed $2,400 raise per teacher?

called "co-production" holds promise in opening new ideas for spending. Co-production is essentially a mechanism where the beneficiaries participate in the delivery of the services they use. That approach is in contrast to a transaction-based means of service delivery that is executed fully and solely by public agencies.

Several of the examples described earlier involve co-production, such as having parents receive funding and drive their own child to school, or having a student receive a cash incentive to read more. With co-production, those benefiting from the service (families and students in this case) are active agents, not passive beneficiaries. Some places have used co-production to pay parents to help with services for students with disabilities (Pillow, 2018).

In a classic example of co-production (but one that does not involve cash transfers to recipients), some districts send text messages to parents about upcoming tests, missed coursework, or attendance. The hope is that a text will enlist parents in the work of supporting and monitoring their child's learning. One can envision a parent receiving such a text, then ensuring that their child spends some time studying. In other words, the parent is doing some of the work of motivating student behavior. And research suggests that this works. In one study, children whose parents were texted, gained 1 month of additional math progress and had less absenteeism than students whose parents weren't texted (Miller et al., 2016). And the low-cost approach—under $10 per student per year—had more impact on student performance than much costlier and more intensive approaches, researchers found.

The contributions to a child's savings account in San Francisco leverage co-production by triggering parents to help set students on a college track at a young age. Co-op preschools, where parents are expected to supplement paid staff by sharing in classroom work, use the same idea. Editors of a research volume on co-production suggest that it is because of these new processes that co-production "can produce major improvements in outcomes and service quality" (Pestoff et al., 2012).

When new alternatives are surfaced at lower costs, it's helpful to include the savings as part of the "would you rather" options—typically as a benefit to the beneficiaries. Would you (employee) rather have our existing benefits plan or a leaner benefit package and more money for salaries? Would you (parent) rather have all students receive tutoring or leverage the lower-cost texting plan (with some tutoring) and more money in the college savings program?

The "would you rather" discussion requires that any freed-up resources be available alongside the cheaper options. And when the options represent a cut, the same principle applies. Leaders might need to bundle several smaller cuts to create a dollar-equivalent comparison to a larger cut.

Step #3: When Some Options Can't Work for Everyone, Consider Customized Options

Having posed the "would you rather" test to numerous audiences, a common reaction we see is to cite outlier cases where the trade-off can't work. The worry is that the texting program isn't viable since it won't help parents without cell phones or parents with too many competing demands to supervise homework. Or that offering cash instead of transportation isn't fair to parents who don't have the flexibility to take on transporting their own children. And it's true that many of the options suggested here won't work for some beneficiaries or in some locales. But that reminds us that we do not need to view these approaches as an all-or-nothing proposition.

It's exactly that risk-averse thinking that often leads to reliance on the expensive one-size-fits-all models that may need retooling. There are times when school leaders can and should offer a range of services that includes some intended specifically for those not able to benefit from other existing options. Built into the texting program, for example, might be resources for students not benefiting from the texting initiative (e.g., tutoring services, after-school supports, etc.).

Everyone does not need to receive the same services in the same way. We can have different delivery models for different people and their different needs.

School staff also might benefit from customized options. As benefit costs skyrocket, as Chad Aldeman explored in Chapter 2, district employees get few choices about health, life, and dental insurance plans. In most cases, the only options are whether to include family members on the plan or to opt out alto-

> **TEACHERS:**
> **WOULD YOU RATHER HAVE**
>
> a. $14,000 to apply to benefits of your choosing, with any savings added to your salary, or
> b. an equivalent $14,000 spent on a set of district-chosen benefits?

gether. So should all benefit plans be designed to maximize value for a 2nd-year teacher who is single or one who is a 15-year veteran with three kids? Presumably the 2nd-year teacher might make different choices regarding health insurance, life insurance, and sick days than the veteran. Just because one employee needs more life insurance, doesn't mean they all do. But the status quo almost never reflects this reality and instead gives everyone a standard package regardless of whether they'd prefer leaner benefits and more salary.

One analysis shows how districts can contain costs and maximize value to employees (Wepman et al., 2010). Instead of a fixed plan, districts might offer a fixed *dollar* amount, say, $14,000, toward a range of benefit choices. Teachers then can choose the benefit packages that carry the most value for them, knowing that they simply can keep any unused benefit funds. If an employee chooses a leaner set of options totaling $9,000, they keep the remaining $5,000 as salary. A teacher selecting benefits totaling $13,000 pockets only a $1,000 differential. If a teacher wants more than the allotted total, they can take a salary deduction to support that choice. In short, the idea is to allow employees to select the mix of benefits and salary that delivers the maximum value *to them*.[2]

But to take advantage of the "would you rather" test, we need to curb the tendency to overreact to the outlier scenario. Co-production can still succeed even if not all actors (e.g., parents) are willing or able to co-produce.

Step #4: Explore the Value to Those on the Receiving End

Ideally, the "would you rather" test works as a forcing mechanism for getting to the heart of what matters, but only if we take the last step of weighing the alternatives from various perspectives. Without this step, we run the risk of assuming that we understand what matters most to different beneficiaries and we then continue operating our systems (and making investments) based on faulty assumptions about what teachers, parents, and students value. Ideally, beneficiaries get a chance to weigh the costs and consider whether the service in its current form makes sense as compared with some alternative.

There are ways to get feedback without making promises. Facing a $59 million budget cut amounting to roughly $600 per pupil, the San Diego Unified School District launched an online survey for parents that shared a range of budget items and, notably, their costs (Saunders, 2018). Parents could choose among higher and lower priorities, including reducing landscaping services, music, library hours, central services, and the like, to achieve the needed $59 million cut. By including the dollar costs of each option, parents could consider the relative costs and value.

> **PARENTS:**
> **WOULD YOU RATHER**
> **HAVE YOUR CHILD**
>
> a. in a class of 27 students taught by one of the district's most effective teachers receiving a $10,000 bonus, or
> b. in a class of 22 students taught by a teacher of unknown effectiveness and receiving no bonus?

Where leaders are worried about presenting false choices, they might pose the question as a clear hypothetical and ask beneficiaries what they'd do if the money belonged to them. Even if a cash alternative doesn't seem viable, simply engaging in the mental test of weighing a set of cost-equivalent alternatives from the beneficiary's point of view can help put choices in perspective.

In some cases, research has already identified potentially viable cost-equivalent trade-offs. The previously cited Goldhaber research establishes that teachers generally prefer more salary over cost-equivalent investments in other supports, such as smaller class sizes and more aides or prep time. Farkas and Duffett (2012) surveyed parents to choose among cost-equivalent options: Would they rather their child be placed in a class of 27 students "taught by one of the district's best performing teachers" or in a class of 22 students "taught by a randomly chosen teacher." Interestingly, 73% of parents opted for the larger class if it came with a teacher proven to be effective, suggesting that parents will tolerate larger classes if accompanied by more effective teachers. Adding a bonus for those effective teachers taking on larger class sizes turns the trade-off into a cost-equivalent one.

The Farkas and Duffett survey also presented options to cut costs in challenging times. It found more support for closing schools, raising class sizes in music and PE, and freezing salaries, and much less support for shortening the school year, charging student fees, or relying more heavily on virtual learning.

An important caution about surveys: The results are much less useful for the purposes of a "would you rather" test if they don't present cost-equivalent options.[3] And existing surveys rarely do. In fact, even most research on the effectiveness of various investments or interventions doesn't document the cost (Molnar, 2018) and thus misses that last step of informing practitioners about the approach's cost-effectiveness. That's likely to change going forward, as the Institute of Education Sciences is now requiring cost-effectiveness analysis for federally funded projects (Schneider, 2018).

Also important when seeking input is to ensure that the beneficiaries are appropriately segmented to yield maximum insight. Sometimes it will make sense to query all teachers, but if the goal is to retain more junior teachers, that might be a time to zero in on how junior teachers in particular value different options. Similarly, it doesn't make sense to ask parents of students without disabilities how they value expenditures for students with disabilities. But given that the costs of special education have grown steadily, it may be a great time to explore how parents of students with disabilities value their services relative to alternative options.

SOME CAUTIONS WHEN CONSIDERING TRADE-OFFS

As discussed above, some cost-equivalent trade-offs that involve doling out cash have limitations, particularly if the public's interest isn't aligned with the private interest. Beyond that conflict, public leaders may have other worries about engaging in the kinds of trade-offs mentioned here.

Many of these concerns manifest only if the cost-equivalent alternative is seriously considered for implementation. For instance, some have noted rightly that while the alternatives might be cost-equivalent, the transition costs also should be factored in before any decision to switch is made. Also worth considering is what happens if the new alternative doesn't prove successful. When cash is involved, will beneficiaries become reliant on their new cash alternative and be reluctant to switch back? If the trade-off involves beneficiaries owning some part of the service, will leaders be relying on people who may not have the technical expertise that professionals have? Or could monetizing some services erode intrinsic motivation for important efforts that don't come with funding?

This kind of thinking assumes that leaders go a step further than this proposal suggests. The "would you rather" thinking described here urges leaders to *explore* the alternatives as part of exploring cost and value. In many cases, one or more of the alternatives may not be politically, legally, or practically feasible at all. Only where leaders are seriously considering an alternative should they more fully consider the transition costs, contingencies, and various implementation effects.

THE BIGGER CHALLENGE:
CONVINCING THE BUREAUCRACY TO LET GO

"Would you rather" thinking requires loosening the reins on large centralized and entrenched bureaucratic systems that thrive on the model they've built. The system makes decisions about which services to deliver, and students and parents are on the receiving end of those services. There are rules, one-size-fits-all policies, and standard operating procedures that together leave very little wiggle room in how public funds are applied in education. Federal and state laws emphasize a compliance orientation that now permeates every level of the system. Add to that the many stakeholder interests, including those who benefit in myriad ways from the delivery models that exist today. Asking these centers of authority to consider turning over the public funds they oversee to the recipients of these services is anathema to those in control.

But that's why it can be powerful. Systems that have decentralized their finances to schools are already changing the power base. Weighing cost-equivalent options for delivering services is a natural next step. Districts in New York City, Boston, Chicago, Denver, Nashville, and other cities have let go of some of their financial constraints and permitted schools to think more creatively about how best to apply their funds. They use a student-based allocation model, also referred to as a weighted student funding model, such that funds are delivered to schools in dollar increments for the number and type of students they have. While most of these districts still have plenty of financial constraints in place, this kind of budgeting model makes it easier to conceive of services in terms of dollars and students.

Furthermore, there is emerging evidence that shifting spending decisions so that they are closer to the recipients of those services could yield improvements for students. For instance, the shift to greater principal control of resources appears to be linked to improved student outcomes (Mizrav, 2014). Part of what may be happening here is that when those closest to the services (including those receiving the services) are more invested in the spending decisions, that investment actually can *affect* the quality of the services. "Would you rathers" can help promote this engagement in spending decisions.

For most systems, however, a push for "would you rather" thinking likely will be met with inertial pushback. That doesn't mean it isn't worth doing.

WHY NOW IS A PARTICULARLY GREAT TIME TO APPLY "WOULD YOU RATHER" THINKING

School finance is likely to stay in the spotlight for the foreseeable future as education leaders begin grappling with an unprecedented level of school-by-school financial transparency necessitated by the federal Every Student Succeeds Act (ESSA). Of course, it's not just school systems and policymakers that will have access to more per-pupil data than ever before—so will parents, the media, advocacy groups, and the community at large. That means education leaders may face increasingly thorny questions about their spending decisions and practices: Who gets what finite resources, why, and to what effect? Leaders have a timely opportunity to apply "would you rather" thinking to proactively engage and build trust with their communities. Decisions about how best to spend education funding deserve careful attention, especially as budgets become more austere. Toward that end, education leaders have timely opportunities to use the test to do at least three things.

Creatively Grapple with Education's Built-in Cost Escalators

Most public education systems face built-in cost escalators and constrained resources, and with an economic downturn, these constraints may worsen. Thus far, engaging beneficiaries in addressing challenges like ballooning pension debt and retiree health care costs has proven difficult. Using the "would you rather" test to develop cost-equivalent scenarios may help break the gridlock.

For instance, Maria Fitzpatrick's (2015) work demonstrates that Illinois teachers value salary more than comparable investments in their pensions—so much so that they'd accept on average a 20 cent salary increase for each dollar

> **TEACHERS:**
> **WOULD YOU RATHER HAVE**
>
> a. $1,000 in pension benefits (today's value), or
> b. some or all of that cash today?

increase in retirement benefits (at present value). This "would you rather" option could be the basis of new, real-world retirement benefit alternatives that are more financially sustainable in the long run.

In Shelby County Schools in Tennessee, Chief Operating Officer Lin Johnson has proposed swapping retiree health benefits for college debt relief as a way to address crippling costs of retiree medical benefits (Kebede, 2019). Two previous proposals for cuts in retiree health benefits fell flat, but this third attempt came with a "would you rather" alternative and it seems to be gaining traction.

Properly Vet Expansive Proposals for New Investments

Among the many larger proposals swirling about in the policy ether are universal pre-K, free college, dual enrollment, college debt relief, expanded STEM offerings, teacher housing, and social–emotional learning. But without rigorous exploration at the front end, we risk building costly new systems that may not deliver their intended value and yet, once established, are very difficult to redirect.

> **STATE LEGISLATORS:**
> **WOULD YOU RATHER**
>
> a. subsidize excess credits for all students in public higher education, or
> b. expand higher education access to 10,000 more students, producing 2,000 degrees per year in your state?

When presented as ideas, most of these expansion proposals tend to be popular. But reactions are more nuanced when the costs and alternatives are weighed. My team found this when we computed the cost to states of subsidizing excess credits at public universities. Many students and faculty initially favored subsidizing courses that went beyond the degree requirements (Jacobson, 2014). Our research showed that the excess credit subsidies in both Georgia and New York could be used instead to support an additional more than 10,000 students, resulting in the production of 2,000 more degrees per year in each state (Kinne et al., 2013). This and similar research has served to focus attention on how best to apply state subsidies to maximize collective benefit (Complete College America, 2011).

As officials weigh any new investments, it makes sense to consider whether the proposed investments are, dollar for dollar, the best way to leverage a given amount of public money, particularly compared with other ways to spend the funds, including simply doling out cash.

Engage the Public Around Trade-Offs in Ways That Improve Trust

Done thoughtfully, the "would you rather" test actively involves the recipients of a program or service—teachers, parents, and students, among others—in the decisionmaking process. This can increase community engagement and public trust in the system.

We know from messaging research that the public trusts leaders who talk in terms of cost-equivalent trade-offs and dollars, with numbers clearly linked to students and what the dollars will do for students (Council of Great City Schools; Roza & Anderson, 2019). In other words, leveraging the "would you rather" format to engage teachers, parents, and students to collectively make the system stronger works as a communications strategy as well.

SO WOULD YOU RATHER THAT YOUR LEADERS:
A. CONTINUE MAKING FINANCIAL DECISIONS AS USUAL, OR
B. DO THE HARD WORK OF FULLY EXPLORING FINANCIAL TRADE-OFFS?

Public schooling comes with layers of rules, regulations, grant requirements, and the like, which can wind up promoting a compliance mindset around spending decisions. Coupled with the inertia typical of bureaucratic organizations, this can keep education leaders on a spending path even when the costs and value no longer justify it. Used as an ongoing part of routine budget and finance deliberations and functions, "would you rather" thinking lets leaders pause to examine what services have been built (or are proposed), at what cost, for what value, and to whom. It can help leaders think more flexibly about leveraging dollars to do more for students. And it offers leaders a chance to rethink approaches to common challenges.

The "would you rather" approach may well prompt discomfort among education leaders, who generally are not accustomed to monetizing services. But skirting cost discussions can breed distrust and inaccurate assumptions about what real-world trade-offs exist. Rather, if costs are clear and the invitation is open for ideas on how to make the money work harder, communities can deliberate and decide how best to apply the limited resources to do the most for students.

That's a game worth playing.

NOTES

1. Example comes from the author's discussion with the school's leadership.

2. With cafeteria plans, districts and unions negotiate the district's contribution of total benefits per teacher, rather than the level and type of each benefit. Unions might work to arrange a larger set of health plans or other benefits, thereby ensuring that members have access to customized compensation packages that can attract and retain educators.

3. While helpful in providing teachers' feelings on various topics, surveys like the 2018 E4E survey don't quantify options when they ask about stipends, higher salaries, retirement options, etc. See Educators for Excellence (2018).

REFERENCES

Aizenman, N. (2017, August 7). *How to fix poverty: Why not just give people money?* NPR. www.npr.org/sections/goatsandsoda/2017/08/07/541609649/how-to-fix-poverty-why-not-just-give-people-money

Aldeman, C. (2019, May 13). *Money > complicated loan forgiveness programs.* Bellwether Education Partners. www.eduwonk.com/2019/05/money-complicated-loan-forgiveness- programs.html

Bock, J. (2011, November 13). *$100,600 • $79,558 • $63,671 lottery jackpots? Nope. Sick day payouts for teachers.* St. Louis Post-Dispatch. www.stltoday.com/news/local/education/lottery-jackpots-nope-sick-day-payouts-for-teachers/article_272cf07c-780c-5c08-bbf4-b737b67e18bb.html

Bueno, C., & Sass, T. (2018, May 1). *The effects of differential pay on teacher recruitment and retention.* Andrew Young School of Policy Studies. ssrn.com/abstract=3296427

Certificate in Education Finance. (n.d.). Georgetown University McCourt School of Public Policy. mccourt.georgetown.edu/executive-education/certificate-in-education-finance-cef

Chingos, M. M., & Whitehurst, G. J. (2011). *Class size: What research says and what it means for state policy.* Brookings Institution. www.brookings.edu/research/class-size-what-research-says-and-what-it-means-for-state-policy

Complete College America. (2011, September). *Time is the enemy.* www.luminafoundation.org/files/resources/time-is-the-enemy.pdf

Council of Great City Schools. (n.d.). *Supporting effective teaching: Communications resources for implementing new systems for teacher development and evaluation.* www.cgcs.org/cms/lib/DC00001581/Centricity/Domain/90/Effective _Teaching_Comms_Reso urces.pdf

Denver Public Schools. (2017, September 1). *DPS, DCTA reach agreement on contract* [Press release]. www.dpsk12.org/dcta-dps-reach-agreement-on-teacher -employment-contract

Educators for Excellence. (2018). *Voices from the classroom.* e4e.org/sites/default /files/2018_voices_from_the_classroom_teacher_survey.pdf#page=13

Farkas, S., & Duffett, A. (2012, August). *How Americans would slim down public education.* Thomas B. Fordham Institute. http://www.edexcellencemedia.net /publications/2012/20120802-How-Americans-Would-Slim-Down-Public -Education/20120802HowAmericaWouldSlimDownPublicEducationFINAL.pdf

Fitzpatrick, M. (2015, November). How much are public school teachers willing to pay for their retirement benefits? *American Economic Journal: Economic Policy, 7*(4), 165–188.

Fryer, R., Jr. (2010, April). *Financial incentives and student achievement* (NBER Working Paper No. 15898). National Bureau of Economic Research. www .nber.org/papers/w15898.pdf

Futernick, K. (2007). *A possible dream: Retaining California teachers so all students learn.* Sacramento: California State University. www2.calstate.edu/impact-of -the-csu/teacher-education/educator-quality-center/Documents/Futernick%20 2007.pdf

Goldhaber, D., DeArmond, M., & Deburgomaster, S. (2011). Teacher attitudes about compensation reform. *ILR Review, 64*(3), 441–463.

Jacobson, S. (2014, October 13). *UCF students protest higher tuition for "excess" classes.* Orlando Sentinel. www.sun-sentinel.com/news/education/os-ucf-excess -credit-hours-surcharge- 20141009-story.html

Johnson, A. (2019, May 1). *Acuity insurance gets naming rights to the Grafton High School gym.* Milwaukee Journal Sentinel. www.jsonline.com/story/communities /northshore/news/grafton/2019/05/01/acuity-insurance-donates-425-000 -grafton-school-district-district-grants-naming-rights-grafton-hs-gy/3615662002

Kebede, L. (2019, April 18). *To slow rising costs, district wants to help new Memphis teachers pay for college debt instead of retiree benefits.* Chalkbeat. www .chalkbeat.org/posts/tn/2019/04/18/to-slow-rising-costs-district-wants-to-help -new-memphis-teachers-pay-for-college-debt-instead-of-retiree-benefits

Kinne, A., Blume, G., & Roza, M. (2013, May). *The high price of excess credits: How new approaches could help students and schools.* Edunomics Lab. edunomicslab .org/wp- contentloads/2013/05/Edunomics-Lab_RR_Excess-Credits.pdf

Miller, S., Davison, J., Yohanis, J., Sloan, S., Gildea, A., & Thurston, A. (2016, July). *Texting parents: Evaluation report and executive summary.* Education Endowment Foundation. files.eric.ed.gov/fulltext/ED581121.pdf

Mizrav, E. (2014). *Could principal autonomy produce better schools? Evidence from the school and staffing survey.* Washington, DC: Georgetown University.

Molnar, M. (2018, August 27). *What Works Clearinghouse looking at costs of implementing interventions.* Education Week Market Brief. marketbrief.edweek .org/marketplace-k-12/works-clearinghouse-looking-costs-implementing -interventions

National Education Association. (2019, April). *Rankings of the states 2018 and estimates of school statistics 2019*. www.nea.org/assets/docs/2019%20Rankings%20and%20Estimates%20Report.pdf

Nebraska Department of Education. (2017, August 9). *Frequently asked questions: Pupil transportation*. www.education.ne.gov/fos/pupil-transportation/frequently-asked-questions/#reimbursement

Parsons, S. (2018, October 8). *Seattle should do better on pre-K funding*. Crosscut. crosscut.com/2018/10/seattle-should-do-better-pre-k-funding

Pestoff, V., Brandsen, T., & Verschuere, B. (2012). *New public governance, the third sector, and co-production*. Routledge.

Pillow, T. (2018, September 5). *For Brandon: How one family's struggle can help us imagine an education system that does better by exceptional children*. Center on Reinventing Public Education. www.crpe.org/thelens/brandon-one-familys-struggle

Podolsky, A., Kini, T., Bishop, J., & Darling-Hammond, L. (2016, September). *Solving the teacher shortage: How to attract and retain excellent educators*. Learning Policy Institute. learningpolicyinstitute.org/product/solving-teacher-shortage-brief

Roza, M. (2015, November). *Breaking tradition: A fixed-dollar pay raise strategy that benefits teachers and school districts*. Edunomics Lab. https://edunomicslab.org/2015/11/19/fixed-dollar-pay-raise-strategy/

Roza, M., & Anderson, L. (2019, May 21). *Understanding school finance is one thing. Being effective in communicating about it is another skill entirely*. Learning Policy Institute. https://learningpolicyinstitute.org/blog/understanding-school-finance-one-thing-being-effective-communicating-about-it-another-skill

Saunders, M. (2018, January 18). *San Diego Unified asks parents what services should be cut due to budget shortfall*. ABC News San Diego. www.10news.com/news/san-diego-unified-asks-parents-what-services-should-be-cut-due-to-budget-shortfall

Schneider, M. (2018, September 5). *Message from IES director: Changes are coming to research competitions*. Institute of Education Sciences. ies.ed.gov/director/remarks/researchcomp2018.asp

Teoh, M. & Coggins, C. (2012). *Great expectations: Teachers' views on elevating the teaching profession*. TeachPlus. https://www.classsizematters.org/wp-content/uploads/2012/11/1350917768_Teach-Plus-Great-Expectations-1.pdf

Wepman, N., Roza, M., & Sepe, C. (2010, December 9). *The promise of cafeteria-style benefits for districts and teachers*. Center on Reinventing Public Education. www.crpe.org/sites/default/files/rr_crpe_Benefits_Dec10_0.pdf

Wolfman-Arent, A. (2018, September 24). *Philly's $40,000 cab ride, and what it says about modern, urban education*. WHYY Radio. whyy.org/articles/phillys-40000-cab-ride-and-what-it-says-about-modern-urban-education

CHAPTER 6

Rethinking School Staffing

Bryan Hassel and Emily Ayscue Hassel

INTRODUCTION

In any discussion of resource allocations or budget revisions in public education, the "staffing" line item looms large. That's partly because of the sheer magnitude of spending on school staff within the budget: Of the $596 billion in operating expenditures in U.S. public schools for 2015–2016, $476.5 billion—or 80%—went to employee salaries and benefits.[1] With 6.5 million employees, 3.2 million of whom are teachers, the public education system runs on people (U.S. Department of Education, 2019b).

Staffing also looms large because of the enormous impact that educators have on student learning. The effectiveness of teachers is well known as the most important school-based driver of student learning, with the effectiveness of school principals in second place.[2] If schools do an exemplary job of allocating resources for staffing, they have a better shot at providing a high-quality education to all of their students. If they allocate staffing resources badly, they leave students far behind their potential and fail to achieve the mission of education.

The crushing reality is that since 1970, U.S. public education per-pupil spending increased approximately 145% in real terms, yet teacher pay was nearly flat, increasing just 7.5% in real terms. Working hours went up even more, though, according to the federal *Schools and Staffing Survey* (U.S. Department of Education, National Center for Education Statistics, 2017, 2018b)—meaning that teacher pay per hour actually declined (Perie et al., 1997). If classroom teacher pay had increased in proportion to spending since 1970, then average annual teacher pay would be nearly $140,000 today, instead of less than half that.

Among other costs, new dollars flowed into many more jobs. Schools reduced student–teacher ratios by adding more teachers, but that did not proportionately lower typical class sizes, for many people in new "teaching" positions do not actually teach classrooms of students. Instead, most perform assisting roles, such as instructional interventionist or data coach. Some additions were important for the extreme differentiation needed to help all students learn—teachers to help English language learners and students with special needs. But few of the other new roles, although intended to help classroom teachers succeed, came with clear authority, time for classroom teachers to learn from them, selectivity for teaching prowess, significant extra pay, or accountability for student-learning growth.

Therefore, despite the many new positions, schools today overwhelmingly use the same basic "one-teacher, one-classroom" staffing model, with all teachers reporting to the principal and working largely alone. While other professions have evolved to organize professionals into small teams and offer paid career advancement for people leading those teams, teaching jobs—not just pay—have remained generally stagnant.

After decades of stubborn achievement gaps and disappointing levels of improvement in student learning, it is time to reconsider how public education spends money on people.

In this chapter, we explore data illuminating these mistakes of the past, our vision for a very different future, and key steps to achieve the vision.[3] At the core of this vision is the creation of well-paid, high-authority, high-accountability, small-team leadership by excellent teachers—those who previously have produced high-growth student learning—who continue to teach students part of the time.

If implemented at large scale, these "multi-classroom leader" (MCL) roles and other staffing changes that make them possible can provide multiple benefits, including paid residencies for all educators, salaries more competitive with other professions, secure retirement funding, routine on-the-job development, and better student learning—all within regular budgets. Further reallocation of district- and state-level spending would put even more dollars into teachers' pockets, reversing decades of resources shifting away from teacher pay.

FOR 5 DECADES, A PROFESSION LEFT BEHIND

With the benefit of hindsight, we can see that after the 1969–1970 school year, the United States was about to usher in decades of rising real per-pupil spending on K–12 education. In that year, our public schools spent $5,360 per pupil on "current expenditures" (operating budgets, not including capital) in 2017–2018 dollars. By 2015–2016, they were spending $13,319, a real increase of 145% (U.S. Department of Education, 2017). In part, this rise reflected the country's laudable increased commitment to educating students with special needs and the growing share of English language learners. At the same time, it signaled a nation willing to boost its investment in an increasingly important public good—an educated citizenry. But this era of increase proved to be an era of wage stagnation for the teaching profession. Many more got hired, yes, but system, policy, and union leaders let teachers'

real hourly pay decline, and they allowed teaching to miss the wave of innovation that infused other professions with well-paid career advancement
opportunities, especially for women.

As increasing funds flowed into the system, education leaders chose how
to spend the new dollars. They could have focused on attracting high-poten-
tial classroom teachers and helping them get even better: raising their base
pay, developing them on the job, and offering opportunities to advance for
more pay, thereby making teaching a career competitive with law, medicine,
and other professions that increasingly attracted top college graduates—
men and women alike.

Yet education leaders took a different route. Instead of investing in classroom teachers, they hired many more people while keeping educator pay flat.
They provided inconsistent professional development led by people who no
longer taught. And the forms of advancement they offered generally required
leaving the classroom.[4]

The numbers are stark. Real education spending grew at 19 times the
rate of real average teacher pay, as shown in Figure 6.1 (U.S. Department of
Education, 2018b). Since teacher work hours per week rose, teacher pay per
hour actually declined over that time.[5] Even if teacher pay had garnered just
55% of the overall increase, the average teacher would have earned a six-

**Figure 6.1. Percent Change in Real Per-Pupil U.S. Education Spending and Real
Average Teacher Pay, 1969–1970 to 2015–2016**

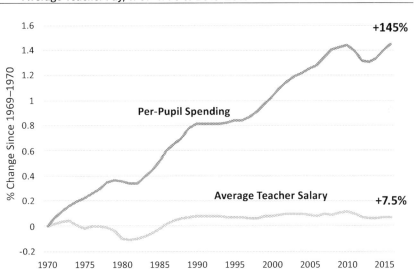

Source: U.S. Department of Education, National Center for Education Statistics (2017,
2018b).

figure salary in 2015–2016. But while 50.8% of all U.S. K–12 spending went to teacher salaries in 1969–1970, that figure was just 30.9% in 2015–2016.[6] The United States shifted from spending more than half of its K–12 dollars on teachers to spending less than one-third. While 80% of dollars still went to "personnel," a dwindling share of this went into teachers' pockets.

Leaders instead added more nonteaching staff in district offices and schools. The added costs were (hindsight tells us) largely for ineffective strategies to shore up a teaching profession that struggled to compete well in the intensifying market for talent. In that market, the chance to learn, advance, and earn more won over top performers across professions.

From 1969 to 2016, public school enrollment rose from approximately 42 million to 47 million students, an increase of 12.7% (U.S. Department of Education, 2018a). Yet real per-pupil spending on "other school services" went up more than eightfold. Administration quadrupled. Plant operations tripled. Spending on all "instruction" costs doubled, but that category included many expenses other than teacher pay (U.S. Department of Education, 2018c). In other words, states and districts went on a spending spree benefitting nearly everything and everyone—except classroom teachers and most students.

Figure 6.2. Percentage Increase in Categories of U.S. Public Education Staff Between 1969-1970 and 2015-2016

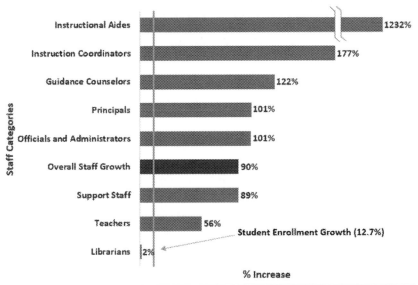

Source: U.S. Department of Education, National Center for Education Statistics (2019b).

Indeed, the number of "support staff" rose by 89.6%—seven times the rate of enrollment growth. The number of instructional coordinators went up 177%, 14 times the rate of enrollment growth. And employment of instructional aides rose at nearly 100 times the rate of enrollment growth. The number of teachers increased, too, by 56%, more than four times the rate of enrollment growth. In 1969, the United States employed 2 million teachers, about one for every 22 students. By 2015–2016, schools had 3.2 million teachers, one for every 16 pupils (U.S. Department of Education, 2019b). But class sizes did not decline accordingly. Class-size estimates date back only to the late 1980s, when the average classroom had about 24 students (U.S. Department of Education, 2000). By 2015, the average class size was 21 students, a decrease of only 12.5% (OECD, 2019). Figure 6.2 shows the figures for all staff categories in the federal data.

HOW TEACHING COMPARED WITH OTHER PROFESSIONS

These numbers were driven in part by the nation's laudable and intensifying commitment to serving students with disabilities in public schools. Special education typically features smaller classes and more aides. Federally supported special education program enrollment increased from 8.3% of all students in 1976–1977 to 13.2% in 2015–2016. Yet this shift does not explain the massive changes in overall staffing levels.[7]

Instead, overall staffing shifts reflected the broader personnel strategy that U.S. education and political leaders adopted for decades: *hiring more people rather than paying people more*. Despite much political talk about higher teacher pay, negligible increases did not account for the growing complexity and hours required for teaching as the public began, rightly, to expect teachers to achieve higher standards with *all* of their students. In essence, the job expectations rose while the compensation didn't. Because teacher pay stayed low relative to other professions that increasingly were attracting talent, schools faced little chance of competing for a larger portion of top college graduates. This was a period in which women, who made up (and still do) the majority of the teaching force, increasingly gained access to other professions. In 1970, women made up 4% of attorneys in the United States (Bowman, 2009). By 2017, they constituted about 35% of lawyers (American Bar Association, 2017). During that same period, the representation of women among accountants doubled, while quadrupling among doctors (Guerra & Huset, 2008; Strasser, 2012; U.S. Department of Labor, 2017).

Rather than increasing salaries to compete for talent, schools aimed to support the teachers who still entered the field by increasing the size of school staffs. In theory, by boosting the number of teachers, schools could keep student loads lower and more manageable. In addition, by adding other staff, including aides and a raft of coaches, instructional coordinators, and the like, schools could help their teachers succeed by supplementing their skills with other people. This approach undoubtedly seemed reasonable to well-intentioned people at all levels.

It also appealed to powerful constituencies. Educators' associations benefited from a growing, dues-paying education workforce. District and state administrators had larger and larger organizations under their purview, one measure of success in any sector. Education schools were able to enroll more students. And, of course, many individuals obtained school jobs that would not have existed had the nation taken a different course.

Although these constituencies undeniably benefited, classroom teachers and students were left holding the bag. For one thing, the large increases in staffing (and other line items) left only pocket change to raise teacher pay, as detailed above. As a result, schools became less effective at attracting top college graduates into their classroom ranks. By the 2000s, only 23% of new teachers and just 14% of those in high-poverty schools were coming from the top third of college classes (Auguste et al., 2010). Between 1963 and 2000, the proportion of new female teachers coming from top-tier colleges dropped from 5% to 1%, while the proportion coming from bottom-tier colleges rose from 16% to 36% (Hoxby & Leigh, 2005). Of course, many highly talented people from a range of colleges entered teaching during this time, and still do today, and being a great college student is not the only qualification for being a great teacher. However, in an era marked by increasing competition for top talent, schools fared worse than they could have by paying all teachers more and, perhaps, paying excellent teachers even more.

What's more, taking this route meant that teaching skipped the staffing innovation that was the hallmark of professional organizations in the second half of the 20th century. Other professions were diversifying their ranks, changing in structure, and developing career paths that let their members make progress while continuing to practice their crafts.

Consider law firms: By the late 20th century, most law firms with staffs the size of schools (or larger) had developed a differentiated career structure in which lawyers entered as junior associates, and then had the opportunity to move up the ranks, becoming senior associates, junior partners, and senior partners (Samuelson, 1990). Importantly, even as they moved up, they continued to practice law—representing clients and trying cases. Even "managing partners"—lawyers who took on the most significant administrative duties—still typically practiced law at least a third of the time (Hagedorn et al., 1989, as cited in Samuelson, 1990, p. 652). Supported by paraprofessionals, legal aides, and other staff, they could focus on the parts of the job that required their professional skills and judgment. Firms invested in technology that helped them do their work more efficiently and effectively. Legal professionals typically worked in teams, with a more accomplished attorney supervising and developing less-seasoned lawyers and support staff in handling each client and case. Professional firms in other sectors, such as accounting and consulting, developed similar structures.

Schools, by contrast, remain organized in what some scholars have called the "egg-crate" or "one-teacher, one-classroom" model (Tyack, 1974). Teachers work largely alone, taking full responsibility for students in their class or classes. Collaboration among them is minimal, typically arising when teachers initiate it or as part of "collaboration-lite" professional learning communities, but not an expected part of the routine school day, except for relatively rare instances of "team teaching." Teachers have opportunities to advance—but only by giving up teaching to coach, becoming administrators, or leaving the profession altogether for more pay.[8] Teachers who remain in the classroom keep doing pretty much the same job over their entire careers. Those who excel at helping students learn reach no more students than other teachers and have no authority to guide their colleagues.

Compensation patterns in teaching also continue to differ substantially from those in other professions that compete for talent. Economist Jacob Vigdor (2008) analyzed the timing of advancement through pay levels by age of physicians, lawyers, and teachers, using data from the American Community Survey. In all three professions, newly entering practitioners earn substantially less than professionals with more experience. In law and medicine, ascent up the pay scale is rapid. The average lawyer reaches "peak earnings" by age 35; the average physician by 40. Teachers, in contrast, must wait until *age 55* on average to reach peak earnings. Law and medicine have created career paths and compensation structures designed to attract and keep talented professionals. But the vast majority of schools continue to use a "steps and lanes" system in which all teachers slowly progress in pay as they attain experience ("steps") and advanced degrees ("lanes") and in which the job of teacher remains much the same throughout one's career.

We say "the vast majority" because there are exceptions. On two occasions, the organization we lead, Public Impact, has been commissioned to find examples of public schools that deviate from the norms. One was a report we developed for the Center for American Progress, *Beyond Classroom Walls* (Kowal & Brinson, 2011). The other was a collaboration with the Clayton Christensen Institute that produced the report *Innovative Staffing to Personalize Learning* (Barrett & Arnett, 2018). In both cases, we conducted extensive searches for examples of schools or school systems that departed from the typical one-teacher, one-classroom model and achieved strong results. With 99,000 public schools, one would think examples of innovative staffing would be easy to find, not needles in the proverbial haystack. In both cases, we did find some: two in the case of *Beyond Classroom Walls*, and eight in the more recent *Innovative Staffing to Personalize Learning*. Needles indeed! It was evident in both searches that the cases we found were outliers; almost all teachers still work in an egg-crate system with traditional steps and lanes compensation.

ALTERNATIVE ATTEMPTS TO IMPROVE TEACHING EFFECTIVENESS

As demands rose on district leaders to educate all students, they knew they must provide more of their pupils with high-quality instruction. They did so not by competing more effectively for classroom teaching talent or reorganizing the career for effectiveness and attractiveness. Instead, they aimed to help by shoring up and backstopping the teaching job. Here we focus on two of the key "shoring up" mechanisms: keeping student loads down, and supporting teachers via a growing number of instructional specialists.

Lower Class Sizes[9]

Although between the 1960s and today, class sizes did not drop as much as student–teacher ratios, many states did enact policies to lower class size.[10] The allure of that move is clear: If teachers have fewer students, they can give each one more attention. Their classes will become easier to manage, fostering more learning for all. Some research backs up these notions. One large study in Tennessee found that for any given teacher, a much smaller class size improves student learning in the early grades (Word et al., 1990). From this perspective, dramatically reducing class sizes from the typical mid-20s to the 13 to 17 range has a positive effect on student learning in the K–3 years. (There's no strong evidence of the value of small classes in grades 4 and above.)

Yet lowering student loads has not generated benefits when policymakers scaled up the concept—as many did over recent decades. Florida spent billions on class-size reductions with no positive impact on student results. A statewide study of Connecticut elementary schools found no statistically significant impact of class sizes (Chingos, 2013; Hoxby, 2000). These were well-intended, reasonable policy efforts. So why did they fall short of proponents' hopes? Because large-scale reductions in student loads required hiring thousands more teachers nationwide, which entailed hiring more people less selectively from the applicant pool, resulting in a lower average effectiveness of teachers. This in effect *reduced* the percentage of students who had excellent teachers—the kind who produce more than a year's worth of academic growth in their pupils each year, which is necessary to close proficiency gaps and help students leap ahead. It also increased the percentage of students with ineffective teachers—the kind who induce far less than a year's worth of student-learning growth.

It appears that the learning value gained through smaller classes may be offset by the dip in the average effectiveness of teachers.

Swelling Ranks of Instructional Specialists

Education leaders also aimed to shore up the teaching force by employing more and more instructional specialists. These individual roles go by different names in different systems: coaches, facilitators, coordinators, specialists, and the like. The hope was that these professionals, by providing professional development and coaching to willing teachers, could help teachers become more effective. As noted above, the ranks of one category of such personnel—what the federal data call "instructional coordinators"—increased 14 times more than the growth in student enrollment between 1969 and 2016 (U.S. Department of Education, 2019b).

These roles, as implemented, have not had their intended impact. Although their ranks expanded dramatically in percentage terms, the number of instructional coordinators was still below 88,000 in 2015–2016. By simple arithmetic, that means schools had one of these professionals for every 36 teachers. Even if just half the schools had coordinators, that would mean one for every 18 teachers. That is a massive "span" relative to what is recommended by management experts. When the business consulting firm Bain & Company looked at this in 2016, it found that a "typical manager of complex, highly skilled work (HR, accounting)" had *approximately five* direct reports. Even a "typical supervisor of low-skilled work (call center, janitorial)" could expect a span of about 15. Instructional coordinators, by contrast, were supposed to boost the effectiveness of about three to seven times the number of people a manager of complex work (like teaching) would expect, and more than twice the number a supervisor of low-skilled work would handle.

Research on this form of support also casts doubt on its efficacy—especially with that kind of span and when implemented at a national scale. Instructional specialists have two main mechanisms for boosting teacher effectiveness: professional development delivered to groups of teachers, and coaching delivered to individual teachers. The research on professional development to groups of teachers (for example, in workshops) is quite discouraging.[11] Research reviewed in a meta-analysis of 60 studies by Kraft et al., in contrast, indicates that teacher "coaching" can improve teachers' practice while boosting student learning (Kraft et al., 2018). Yet this research also points to why the nation's substantial investment in instructional support has not paid off: The value of coaching diminishes substantially when coaching programs are "large." We place "large" in quotes because Kraft et al. define "large" as programs including more than 100 teachers.[12] The effect on student achievement of such programs helping more than 100 teachers is one-third that of programs serving fewer than 100 teachers. Kraft et al. hypothesized that in larger programs it is hard to find enough great coaches, and teacher buy-in diminishes.

In short, over the past few decades, the United States failed to invest in the most important school-level influence on student learning: its classroom teachers. And its efforts to backstop teachers by adding nonteaching staff to schools did not achieve the desired results. Looking ahead to the next half-century, how can education leaders allocate resources much differently and achieve a different outcome?

A BETTER FUTURE

In this section, we share an alternative vision of a better future for the teaching profession. First, we outline what a different pattern of resource allocation at the school, district, and state levels could look like—one that is financially sustainable at scale, and that makes teaching highly competitive for talent and organized to support widespread instructional excellence. Then we explore paths that districts and schools could take to reach that better future, and how state policy could encourage such a transition.

Allocating Resources to Support Great Teaching

How could resources be allocated differently to produce better outcomes? The answer must start with rethinking school "staffing models."

Table 6.1 provides our vision of such a model, which we call "Opportunity Culture." In place of solo teachers receiving light support from a specialist with a wide span, the model engages teachers in small collaborative teams (typically five to six teachers), each led by a proven excellent teacher; these multi-classroom leaders (MCLs) keep their skills fresh by continuing to teach part of the time while providing intensive instructional guidance and coaching to the team. In addition, schools can help teachers on the teams reach more students without increasing instructional group sizes—by adding advanced paraprofessionals to teams (as in other professions). These advanced assistants can help with small-group instruction, supervise students' skills practice and project time, and provide individual tutoring. In place of a flat career, the model offers varied, well-paid career paths. Teachers can take responsibility for more students' learning, with the best reaching the most students, and far more teachers can excel by receiving frequent guidance and development. Resident teachers-in-training can spend a full year as entry-level teachers or advanced paraprofessionals, working under skilled team leaders who have a record of high-growth student learning—while earning full salaries and benefits. Revamped schedules, along with the extra paraprofessional support, provide time during the school day for teaching teams to collaborate and improve. In contrast to "teacher career ladders" that states and districts have implemented in the past, this model is not just seniority-based progression up a ladder. Instead, it creates wholly new roles for teachers to become fully accountable, well-paid team leaders with the time and authority to lead while continuing to teach part of the time.

Our organization created this Opportunity Culture model, now used by more than 300 schools nationally, with over 100 more signed up to use it, numbers that have grown approximately 50% annually since inception in 2013–2014.[13] Innovative staffing models are under development elsewhere as well. For example, in Brooklyn Laboratory Charter Schools, a combination of lead teachers and specialists, resident teachers, and a new-teacher

Table 6.1. Traditional vs. Opportunity Culture Staffing Model

One-Teacher, One-Classroom Model	Opportunity Culture Principles *Teams of teachers and school leaders choose models to:*
Minimal advanced roles that do exist are nonselective, volunteer roles.	***Principle #1: Reach more students and schools with excellent teachers and their teams.*** Excellent teachers reach more students directly or by leading teams while continuing to teach part of the time. Multi-classroom leaders are selected based on prior high learning growth of students and leadership competencies.
Minimal advanced roles that do exist are nonpaying or low-paying.	***Principle #2: Pay teachers more for extending their reach.*** Schools pay multi-classroom leaders supplements averaging 20% of base pay and up to 50%. Schools pay smaller supplements to all teachers who extend their reach and in some cases pay paraprofessionals more.
When advanced roles are better-paying, they often are funded by temporary grants.	***Principle #3: Fund pay within regular budgets.*** Supplements are funded by recurring school-level budgets, not grants, temporary budget line items, or district line items. Supplements are funded by trading positions or other costs, in most cases through natural attrition.
Traditional school schedule provides minimal time for collaboration and leadership.	***Principle #4: Provide protected in-school time and clarity about how to use it for planning, collaboration, and development.*** Teachers responsible for more students have more time to plan. Team leaders and team members have commonly scheduled time at several points weekly during school hours to plan, collaborate, observe, and provide feedback; paraprofessional support and careful scheduling allow this. Scheduled teaching, planning, and collaboration time is strongly protected from interruptions and interfering duties.
Specialists and coaches are not responsible for student learning and have little authority.	***Principle #5: Match authority and accountability to each person's responsibilities.*** Teachers and multi-classroom leaders are formally accountable, matched to the students and subjects they reach. A person's formal authority matches their role, responsibilities, and accountability.

corps play differentiated roles on teams designed to enhance the student experience (Public Impact & Clayton Christensen Institute, 2018). Brooklyn Lab was one of eight examples of innovative staffing highlighted in a report issued by the Christensen Institute and Public Impact (Barrett & Arnett, 2018).

Third-party research shows the impact of Opportunity Culture on student learning. Researchers from the Brookings Institution and American Institutes for Research working through the National Center for Analysis of Longitudinal Data in Education Research (CALDER) studied teachers who produced, on average, 50th-percentile student-learning gains before joining a team led by a multi-classroom leader. After joining an MCL team, they produced learning gains equivalent to those of teachers in the 75th to 85th percentile in math and nearly that high in reading in six of seven statistical models (Backes & Hansen, 2018).

Clearly, significant changes in resource allocation are necessary to make shifts like these happen. In the Opportunity Culture model, the average teacher earns more than today's non-Opportunity Culture teachers, and teachers who take on leadership roles are earning substantial supplements. How do schools pay for it?

Critically, *school teams* that include teachers and the principal choose how to reallocate each school's budget to meet their school's needs. In some schools, funds that have been used to add staff for instructional support are repurposed to pay teachers more in the redesigned staffing model. Typically, schools reallocate funds when positions become vacant, adding more MCL roles over 2 to 3 years. Instead of relying on thinly spread coaches to provide light support, schools use funds to pay more to multi-classroom leaders and their team members, the people with the most direct impact on students.

Second, some Opportunity Culture schools replace a small number of teaching positions with advanced paraprofessional support, as in other professions. These paraprofessionals meet a higher selection bar than the average "teacher's assistant," demonstrating their competence to work with students and assist teams of teachers in achieving ambitious learning goals. They not only save teachers time for more instructional planning and collaboration, but they also cost less. Again, schools typically make these swaps when a teaching position is vacant, especially when a vacancy will be hard to fill well. School teams then reallocate the difference in cost between a teacher and a paraprofessional position to pay supplements to multi-classroom leaders, and sometimes to all of the team's teachers. Some schools also pay their advanced paraprofessionals more. One such position swap funds substantially higher pay for all educators on a grade or subject team of four adults. Schools keep any preexisting assistants, as well. Thus, roughly the same number of adults serve the students, and average instructional group sizes remain approximately the same. In addition, several recent meta-analyses have found that paraprofessionals are actually more effective than the average teacher at raising student achievement via small-group and one-on-one tutoring.[14] Schools could make such "swaps" without fear of a negative impact on students, especially when a multi-classroom leader who has a record of prior high-growth student learning determines each adult's role and leads the team.

School-level staffing shifts are just one step toward paying teachers their due. The same thinking applies to district- and state-level education costs. While Opportunity Culture states and districts have not yet tapped these sources, the same logic applies: Positions and other expenditures added over prior decades to support teachers in ways that have not actually helped them teach more effectively can be reallocated to pay more to teachers, multi-classroom leaders, advanced assistants, principals, and even "multi-school leaders." The potential list of reallocations is long and one best developed with teachers' input, as the Opportunity Culture school staffing changes were.

The net effect of combined school, district, and state funding shifts would be an educator workforce that is higher-paid overall and has greater opportunities for teachers to earn substantially more by first excelling as professionals and then taking on more responsibility. Teaching would resemble more closely the positive aspects of other professions, making it more attractive as a career for all, especially those who accurately believe they will excel as instructional leaders.

In addition, the redesigned staffing model may offer collateral benefits:

- *Giving teachers what they want.* These new models provide varied, paid career advancement opportunities, on-the-job development, and more collaboration—three things that surveys report teachers want.[15]
- *Opportunities for principals.* When schools are redesigned around teacher-led teams, principals can refocus their leadership on leading a "team of leaders" made up of grade and subject team leaders, rather than trying to assume the impossible task of being an "instructional leader" for 20 to 50 individual teachers. With these teams in place, highly effective principals can become "multi-school leaders," creating a similar career path for principals that lets them remain close to schools while earning more and having greater impact—within regular budgets (Public Impact, 2014–2019; E. A. Hassel & B. C. Hassel, 2016).
- *Opportunities for aspiring teachers.* Multi-classroom leader roles are already designed to provide frequent guidance, observation, feedback, and on-the-job coaching by excellent teachers. Aspiring teachers who take either advanced paraprofessional roles or new-teacher positions on these teams can earn full salaries and benefits, within school budgets, while obtaining degrees or certification—making paid residencies the norm (Dean et al., 2016).

Making certification more affordable through within-budget paid residencies, in turn, may increase the diversity of entering teachers, which research has found to benefit students (Egalite et al., 2015).

- *Keeping instructional support functions connected to classroom excellence.* State and district instructional support functions, such as curriculum and professional development, would be more effective if staffed by excellent teachers in hybrid roles modeled on the multi-classroom leader role.

- *Addressing the pension challenge.* As schools make the position trades described here, the potential savings may be large enough to do more than raise teacher pay; schools also could reallocate a portion of saved funds to address the looming crisis of underfunded retirement systems—or to secure the retirements of those currently teaching. That, along with other changes, such as reducing the retirement penalty teachers face when moving across state lines, could further increase the attractiveness of the teaching profession.

Whatever the current level of spending, education leaders can reverse the multi-decade shift of funding away from teacher pay. Could the average base pay of teachers be six figures, within regular budgets? With the changes described here, most likely yes.

Making the Transition

Today's staffing model and resource allocation patterns have been decades in the making. How could U.S. schools move toward a better model? Many features of the current model emerged from state mandates, such as state-wide class-size limits and state funding for instructional coaches or specialists. States likewise could mandate a shift to a new model, but the risk of doing so would be high. Shifts like these require educators to substantially change their ways of working, and these resource changes require trade-offs that have a real impact on individuals. It also would take a big shift in public and parental expectations regarding what schools look like and how they operate. As the number of schools using new staffing models grows, there is a strong argument for making individual schools the locus of decisionmaking about how to make school-level shifts, within principles or guidelines based on research about what works. Educators in schools are in the best position to decide which trade-offs to make, how to phase changes in, and other key choices for each school. Research can guide them with data about what parameters achieve the best student learning and teacher satisfaction.

While teachers have been among the warmest responders to Opportunity Culture staffing models, district and state staff may view change differently. Policymakers may need to reconsider how funding flows, possibly with schools (rather than districts) as the primary funding recipients. No doubt, as they have with school-level financial decisions, a team that included respected teachers and principals in each district and state could make good decisions about resource allocation that better supported instructional excellence. District and state leaders may not be the only ones who struggle to change: Some school principals also might lack the will or capacity to oversee schools with empowered teacher leaders. Enabling the best to become multi-school leaders could address this challenge.

Roles for State Policymakers

First, state policymakers could *set goals* for allocating resources to support great teaching. Goals might include achieving average teacher pay of $100,000, indexed for inflation, within a stated time and increasing the proportion of spending that goes to teacher compensation—aiming for something closer to the 51% of budgets that classroom teachers earned in 1970. States then could track and report how schools, districts, and the state were doing against these goals.

Second, states could *provide funding for transition costs*. Moving to a new model is challenging, requiring multifaceted technical work, such as revamping budgets and schedules, redesigning staff selection and evaluation processes, and the process-organizing aspects of change management. Districts, schools, and states need help to make these complex changes. Funding must come with strong parameters, or else leaders will continue to spend money as they have for decades, on ineffective and unsustainable changes. Parameters might include something like the Opportunity Culture Principles for reallocations at all levels, forcing funding shifts into roles that support instructional excellence and attractive career options. Both Indiana and North Carolina have enacted legislation to fund support for such district- and school-level design, and Arkansas's Department of Education is doing so through the state's ESSA plan.

These two changes alone would help create a labor market in which districts have to compete to provide the conditions, including pay, that attract and retain excellent educators and spread their impact.

Third, state policymakers could *remove policy barriers* that make new staffing models more challenging to implement. Most of the barriers to enacting new staffing models are barriers of the mind or temporary transition "humps" to get over. Still, some states have policy constraints that make it more challenging for schools and districts to redesign staffing. Examples include line-item budgets that limit reallocation: some states would need to revamp funding formulas or allow flexibility via waivers to enable the necessary reallocations. Rigid class-size limits make it difficult for teams of teachers and paraprofessionals to collectively serve a group of students, even when a proven, excellent teacher is taking responsibility. And constraints on the roles paraprofessionals can play can create challenges. In essence, these policies lock in one-teacher, one-classroom structures. In such cases, policymakers could clear the way for schools to make the shift. They could tie flexibility to progress toward the goals and parameters outlined above so that schools use flexibility to create a more attractive, well-supported teaching profession (Public Impact, 2014–2019). Not all constraints lie at the state level; districts also would have to make significant changes in how they work. States also could incentivize districts to lift the barriers put in place by their own policies or provisions in collective-bargaining agreements.

Finally, states can *collect and disseminate data about what works.* As schools, districts, and states adopt new models that put teachers at the center of their profession, some models will thrive, others will stumble, and many will experience the varied mix of results typical in any complex change process. States are in a position, directly or by engaging external parties, to collect data about what works and to change policies in line with lessons learned. By closely monitoring staffing and resource allocation changes, how educators perceive the changes, and what factors correlate with student learning growth, states could gain knowledge that shapes the guidelines for future innovations.

RISK AND REWARD

Moving to different staffing models at scale is not without risks. One is the risk that if schools realize savings through new models, some policymakers may seize the opportunity to cut education budgets. While this risk is impossible to completely mitigate, some of the approaches described above could help. Making schools and their budgets the locus of change and the recipients of more direct funding, for example, disperses the savings in a way that makes it less easily seized.

Another political risk relates to the possibility of these changes being construed as "cutting jobs." While the changes we are envisioning likely would not entail a significant reduction in the number of adults in schools, they would mean shifting the composition of positions in some ways: fewer nonteaching instructional specialists, for example, and more advanced paraprofessionals playing roles that research suggests they are better at than teachers. Districts may have fewer staff, though, while school staff earn far more than today. These changes could be controversial. The most promising way to address this is by using vacancies as the primary mode of transition. Schools and districts will not need to remove people from jobs if, over 2 to 3 years, they use funding freed by newly vacated positions to make staffing changes. If educators' associations indexed their dues on staff pay, shifting resources into teachers' pockets would leave associations no worse off in the bargain and encourage them to endorse a higher-paid profession with better support and career opportunities.

Finally, any complex change like this will encounter instances of poor implementation. The key is how state and district leaders anticipate and respond to inevitable variability. If they follow the all-too-common pattern of letting implementation run for years without scrutiny, they will see the all-too-common bell curve of quality. If they respond, as described in the previous section, by establishing systems to monitor implementation and outcomes, learn from variability, and support schools in improving future iterations based on those lessons, they could institute a virtuous cycle of ever-better opportunities for teachers and their students. Unlike with some reforms, district leaders likely will not have to drag unwilling schools along: Since teachers stand to gain substantially from the changes, schools will not want to miss out on the chance to compete for great teaching talent by offering these roles.

For a sector that depends fundamentally on people, especially class-room teachers, these risks are worth taking. The alternative is to remain locked into today's model, which has left teaching ranked too low among professions in support, advancement opportunity, and pay. Policymakers, pundits, and advocates frequently call on the nation to increase the prestige of and respect for the teaching profession. Yet saying "we respect teachers" will not make it true. Only by reallocating resources to educators directly responsible for students in the ways described here will the nation finally put its money where its mouth is.[16]

NOTES

1. We use the term "operating expenditures" to describe noncapital expenses, although NCES often refers to these as "current" expenditures. See U.S. Department of Education, National Center for Education Statistics (2018c).

2. For summaries of this research on teachers, see Goldhaber (2016). On principals, see Leithwood et al. (2004).

3. The vision articulated here draws on previous publications by the authors, including E. A. Hassel and B. C. Hassel (2009, 2013) and B. C. Hassel and E. A. Hassel (2011).

4. See subsequent text and notes for sources of these facts.

5. Historical federal data on teacher work hours go back only to the 1987–88 *Schools and Staffing Survey*, on which teachers reported an average of 40 hours on all school-related activities (both within school hours and otherwise). By the 2011–12 administration of the *Schools and Staffing Survey*, it had risen to 52—an increase of more than 30%. While survey questions changed somewhat (such as asking about the most recent week in 1987–88 and the typical week in 2011–12), the questions were substantially similar, referring to "school-related activities" and clarifying that both school-hours time and outside-of-school-hours time should be counted. See Perie et al. (1997) ; U.S. Department of Education, National Center for Education Statistics (2012).

6. These figures include the salaries of teachers only, not instructional aides.

7. The rise in percentage of students in special education programs who spend the majority of their time in general classrooms also cannot fully explain this shift. See Department of Education, National Center for Education Statistics (2019).

8. For example, a Florida study showed that elementary and middle school teachers who were more effective at raising student achievement, and then left teaching, earned substantially more in their new jobs. See Chingos and West (2012).

9. This section draws on a prior article by the authors. See B. C. Hassel & E. A. Hassel (2017).

10. According to Chingos & Whitehurst (2011), "In recent decades, at least 24 states have mandated or incentivized class-size limits in their public schools."

11. See, for example, Harris and Sass (2011); U.S. Department of Education, Institute of Education Sciences, National Center for Education Evaluation and Regional Assistance (2010, 2016).

12. Just 13 studies in the meta-analysis had 151 or more teachers, and five had 300 or more (Kraft et al., 2018, p. 559).

13. For more details, see www.opportunityculture.org

14. These meta-analyses are summarized in Slavin (2018). See also Baye et al. (2017); Inns et al. (2018); Pellegrini et al. (2018).

15. For one example, see Markow et al. (2013).

16. The authors would like to thank the many people who contributed to this chapter, including the Public Impact team: Beth Clifford, David Gilmore, and Margaret High (for research assistance) and Sharon Kebschull Barrett (for editing), as well as reviewers from Fordham and AEI.

REFERENCES

American Bar Association. (2017). *A current glance at women in the law.* American Bar Association. www.americanbar.org/content/dam/aba/administrative/women /current_glance_statistics_january2017.pdf

Auguste, B., Kihn, P., & Miller, M. (2010). *Closing the talent gap: Attracting and retaining top-third graduates to careers in teaching: An international and market research-based perspective.* McKinsey. mckinseyonsociety.com/downloads /reports/Education/Closing_the_talent_gap.pdf

Backes, B., & Hansen, M. (2018). *Reaching further and learning more? Evaluating Public Impact's opportunity culture initiative.* National Center for Analysis of Longitudinal Data in Education Research. www.mckinsey.com/~/media /mckinsey/industries/social%20sector/our%20insights/closing%20the%20 teaching%20talent%20gap/closing-the-teaching-talent-gap.ashx

Barrett, S. K., & Arnett, T. (2018). *Innovative staffing to personalize learning: How new teaching roles and blended learning help students succeed.* Public Impact & Clayton Christensen Institute. www.christenseninstitute.org/wp-content /uploads/2018/05/innovative-staffing_2018_final.pdf

Baye, A., Lake, C., Inns, A., & Slavin, R. E. (2017, August). *Effective reading programs for secondary students.* Baltimore, MD: Johns Hopkins University, Center for Research and Reform in Education.

Bowman, C. G. (2009). Women in the legal profession from the 1920s to the 1970s: What can we learn from their experience about law and social change. *Cornell*

Law Faculty Publications, Paper 12. scholarship.law.cornell.edu/cgi/viewcontent
.cgi?article=1011&context=facpub

Chingos, M. M. (2013). Class size and student outcomes: Research and policy implications. *Journal of Policy Analysis and Management, 32*(2), 411–438. www
.mattchingos.com/Chingos_JPAM_prepub.pdf

Chingos, M. M., & West, M. R. (2012). Do more effective teachers earn more outside
the classroom? *Education Finance and Policy, 7*(1), 8–43. www.mitpressjournals
.org/doi/abs/10.1162/EDFP_a_00052

Chingos, M. M., & Whitehurst, G. J. (2011). *Class size: What research says and what
it means for state policy.* Brookings Institution. www.brookings.edu/research
/class-size-what-research-says-and-what-it-means-for-state-policy

Dean, S., Hassel, E. A., & Hassel, B. C. (2016). *Paid educator residencies, within
budget: How new school models can radically improve teacher and principal
preparation.* Author. opportunityculture.org/wp-content/uploads/2016/06/Paid
_Educator_Residencies_Within_Budget-Public_Impact.pdf

Egalite, A., Kisida, B., & Winters, M. (2015, January). Representation in the classroom: The effect of own-race teachers on student achievement. *Economics of
Education Review. 45*, 44–52. 10.1016/j.econedurev.2015.01.007.

Goldhaber, D. (2016, Spring). In schools, teacher quality matters most. *Education
Next, 16*(2), 56–62.

Guerra, B. B., & Huset, M. J. (2008). *American Woman's Society of Certified Public
Accountants history 75 years.* AWSCPA. www.aicpa.org/content/dam/aicpa/career
/womenintheprofession/downloadabledocuments/awscpa-75th-anniversary
-journal.pdf

Harris, D. N., & Sass, T. R. (2011). Teacher training, teacher quality and student
achievement. *Journal of Public Economics, 95*(7–8), 798–812. doi.org/10.1016/j
.jpubeco.2010.11.009

Hassel, B. C., & Hassel, E. A. (2011). *Opportunity at the top: How America's best
teachers could close the gaps, raise the bar, and keep our nation great.* Public
Impact. www.opportunityculture.org/2011/12/15/opportunity-at-the-top

Hassel, B. C., & Hassel, E. A. (2017). *One more time now: Why lowering class sizes backfires.* Education Next. www.educationnext.org/one-time-now-lowering
-class-sizes-backfires

Hassel, E. A., & Hassel B. C. (2009). *3X for all: Extending the reach of education's
best.* Public Impact. www.opportunityculture.org/2011/10/31/3x-for-all

Hassel, E. A., & Hassel, B. C. (2013). *An opportunity culture for all: Making
teaching a highly paid, high-impact profession.* Public Impact. https://files.eric
.ed.gov/fulltext/ED560180.pdf

Hassel, E. A., & Hassel, B. C. (2016). *An excellent principal for every school: Trans-
forming schools into leadership machines.* Public Impact. http://opportunity
culture.org/wp-content/uploads/2016/04/An_Excellent_Principal_for_Every
_School-Public_Impact.pdf

Hoxby, C. M. (2000). The effects of class size on student achievement: New evidence from population variation. *The Quarterly Journal of Economics, 115*(4),
1239–1285. academic.oup.com/qje/article-abstract/115/4/1239/1820394

Hoxby, C., & Leigh, A. (2005). Wage distortion. *Education Next, 4*(2). education
next.org/wagedistortion

Inns, A., Lake, C., Pellegrini, M., & Slavin, R. (2018, March). *Effective programs
for struggling readers: A best-evidence synthesis.* Paper presented at the annual

meeting of the Society for Research on Educational Effectiveness, Washington, DC.

Kowal, J., & Brinson, D. (2011). *Beyond classroom walls: Developing innovative work roles for teachers*. Center for American Progress. www.americanprogress .org/issues/education-k-12/reports/2011/04/14/9527/beyondclassroom-walls

Kraft, M. A., Blazar, D., & Hogan, D. (2018). The effect of teacher coaching on in-struction and achievement: A meta-analysis of the causal evidence. *Review of Ed-ucational Research, 88*(4), 547–588. scholar.harvard.edu/mkraft/publications /effect-teacher-coaching-instruction-and-achievement-meta-analysis-causal

Leithwood, K., Seashore, K., Anderson, S., & Wahlstrom, K. (2004). *Review of research: How leadership influences student learning*. Wallace Foundation. www.wallacefoundation.org/knowledge-center/Documents/How-Leadership -Influences-Student-Learning.pdf

Markow, D., Macia, L., & Lee, H. (2013). *The MetLife survey of the American teach-er: Challenges for school leadership*. Metropolitan Life Insurance Company. www.metlife.com/content/dam/microsites/about/corporate-profile/MetLife -Teacher-Survey-2012.pdf

OECD. (2019). Education at a glance: Student–teacher ratio and average class size. *OECD Education Statistics* [Database]. stats.oecd.org/Index.aspx?DataSetCode =EAG_PERS_RATIO

Pellegrini, M., Inns, A., & Slavin, R. (2018, March). *Effective programs in elementa-ry mathematics: A best-evidence synthesis*. Paper presented at the annual meet-ing of the Society for Research on Educational Effectiveness, Washington, DC.

Perie, M., Baker, D. P., & Bobbitt, S. (1997, February). *Time spent teaching core ac-ademic subjects in elementary schools: Comparisons across community, school, teacher, and student characteristics*. nces.ed.gov/pubs/97293.pdf

Public Impact. (2014–2019). *Seizing opportunity at the top II: State policies to reach every student with excellent teaching*. Author. www.opportunityculture.org /2014/10/14/seizing-opportunity-at-the-top

Public Impact & Clayton Christensen Institute. (2018). *Innovative staffing to person-alize learning: Brooklyn laboratory charter schools*. Author. http://publicimpact .com/innovative-staffing-to-personalize-learning/

Samuelson, S. S. (1990). The organizational structure of law firms: Lessons from man-agement theory. *Ohio State Law Journal, 51*, 645–673. kb.osu.edu/bitstream /handle/1811/64072/OSLJ_V51N3_0645.pdf

Slavin, R. (2018, April). *New findings on tutoring: Four shockers*. robertslavinsblog .wordpress.com/2018/04/05/new-findings-on-tutoring-four-shockers

Strasser, A. R. (2012). *Despite growing number of female doctors and lawyers, wom-en's pay still lags behind*. Think Progress. thinkprogress.org/despite-growing -number-of-female-doctors-and-lawyers-womens-pay-still-lags-behind-9b43 f25c0335/

Tyack, D. B. (1974). *The one best system: A history of American urban education* (Vol. 95). Harvard University Press.

U.S. Department of Education, Institute of Education Sciences, National Center for Education Evaluation and Regional Assistance. (2010). *Impacts of compre-hensive teacher induction: Final results from a randomized controlled study* (NCEE 2010-4027). citeseerx.ist.psu.edu/viewdoc/download;jsessionid=36C58 7022134D329B5F5270B6C0BA85A?doi=10.1.1.363.4766&rep=rep1 &type=pdf

U.S. Department of Education, Institute of Education Sciences, National Center for Education Evaluation and Regional Assistance. (2016). *Focusing on mathematical knowledge: The impact of content-intensive teacher professional development* (NCEE 2016-4010). files.eric.ed.gov/fulltext/ED569154.pdf

U.S. Department of Education, National Center for Education Statistics. (2000, December). *Statistical analysis report: Monitoring school quality: An indicators report* (NCES 2001-030). nces.ed.gov/pubs2001/2001030.pdf

U.S. Department of Education, National Center for Education Statistics. (2017, October). Table 236.55: Total and current expenditures per pupil in public elementary and secondary schools: Selected years, 1919–20 through 2015–16. nces .ed.gov/programs/digest/d18/tables/dt18_236.55.asp?current=yes

U.S. Department of Education, National Center for Education Statistics. (2018a, September). Table 203.80: Average daily attendance in public elementary and secondary schools, by state or jurisdiction: Selected years, 1969–70 through 2015–16. nces.ed.gov/programs/digest/d18/tables/dt18_203.80.asp?current=yes

U.S. Department of Education, National Center for Education Statistics. (2018b, September). Table 211.50: Estimated average annual salary of teachers in public elementary and secondary schools: Selected years, 1959–60 through 2017–18. nces.ed.gov/programs/digest/d18/tables/dt18_211.50.asp?current=yes

U.S. Department of Education, National Center for Education Statistics. (2018c). Table 213.10: Staff employed in public elementary and secondary school systems, by type of assignment: Selected years, 1949–50 through fall 2016. nces.ed .gov/programs/digest/d18/tables/dt18_213.10.asp?current=yes

U.S. Department of Education, National Center for Education Statistics. (2018d). Table 236.20: Total expenditures for public elementary and secondary education and other related programs, by function and subfunction: Selected years, 1990–91 through 2015–16. nces.ed.gov/programs/digest/d18/tables/dt18_236 .20.asp?current=yes

U.S. Department of Education, National Center for Education Statistics. (2019a). Fast facts: Students with disabilities. nces.ed.gov/fastfacts/display.asp?id=64

U.S. Department of Education, National Center for Education Statistics. (2019b). Table 213.10: Staff employed in public elementary and secondary school systems, by type of assignment: Selected years, 1949–50 through fall 2016. nces .ed.gov/programs/digest/d18/tables/dt18_213.10.asp?current=yes

U.S. Department of Education, National Center for Education Statistics, Schools and Staffing Survey. (2012). Table 5: Number and percentage of public school teachers who are regular full-time teachers and average number of hours per week that regular full-time teachers spent on selected activities during a typical full week, by state: 2011–12. nces.ed.gov/surveys/sass/tables/sass1112_2013314_t1s_005.asp

U.S. Department of Labor, Bureau of Labor Statistics. (2017). *Labor force statistics from the Current Population Survey, Household data annual averages, Table 11: Employed persons by detailed occupation, sex, race, and Hispanic or Latino ethnicity.* www.bls.gov/cps/aa2017/cpsaat11.htm

Vigdor, J. (2008). Scrap the sacrosanct salary schedule. *Education Next, 8*(2). www .educationnext.org/scrap-the-sacrosanct-salary-schedule

Word, E., Johnston, J., Bain, H. P., Fulton, B. D., Zaharias, J. B., Achilles, C. M., Lintz, M. N., Folger, J., & Breda, C. (1990). *The State of Tennessee's student/teacher achievement ratio (STAR) project.* Tennessee Board of Education. www.class sizematters.org/wp-content/uploads/2016/09/STAR-Technical-Report-Part-I.pdf

Part III

GETTING STARTED

CHAPTER 7

Bridging the Technological Divide (for Good)

How Public Education Leaders Can Successfully Integrate Technology, Without Breaking the Bank

Scott Milam, Carrie Stewart, and Katie Morrison-Reed

As technology becomes ubiquitous in our lives and transforms many industries, school systems often feel drawn—or pressured—to incorporate more of it into the classroom. As one recent survey showed, penetration of mobile devices into the K–12 education market, including iPads and Chromebooks, had increased to over 50% by 2018, with many schools and districts now focusing on device refresh. This study also underscored the fact that "the US [K–12] market remains the largest market by far" for mobile devices, and demand "is forecast to grow throughout 2018 and 2019" (Futuresource Consulting, n.d.). Yet schools often struggle with how to manage this shift financially. What should they be investing in, how much should they invest, and where will the money come from?

The promise is real. Technology can engage students in ways that work best for them, based on their diverse preferences, needs, and capabilities. Teachers can personalize their students' learning experience—customizing content and progressing at a pace suitable to each student. Schools can have immediate access to data that help teachers understand the progress each pupil is making, intervene as needed, and adjust in real time. And as with any major innovation in teaching and learning, the goal is to obtain—and retain—a substantial improvement in student outcomes.

With sound financial planning, the smart incorporation of technology indeed will allow for increased "bang for the educational buck." But when incorporated poorly, technology can distract, detract, and waste a lot of money. Sadly, this happens far too often, in part because it's daunting to commit to and implement transformational change, especially with budgets full of costs that appear fixed and that change little year over year.

Two interlinked challenges, then, face education leaders: identifying the most effective approach to integrating technology in the classroom, including what to prioritize spending on, and how to pay for these investments. This chapter addresses those challenges. We share examples of how school districts have implemented technology with fidelity, what types of resources districts are investing in to scale technology-enabled schools, and how districts are paying for these investments. We also offer suggestions for education leaders to consider as they prepare for these changes in their budgets and spending practices.

What follows is based primarily on our work at Afton Partners, an education finance firm that helps school systems implement strategies that sustain effective education programs. Since 2011, we have worked with over 130 schools, school systems, and school leaders in developing and evaluating long-term resource plans to support innovative school models, including those incorporating technology into the classroom.

Most of the school transformations we have directly assisted have been spurred by competitive grant programs that provided one-time capital to support the implementation of innovative school models, particularly for high-needs students. These grant programs have funded technical supports to help sites identify effective strategies and success metrics. The programs also built a community or cohort of schools so that other sites can learn from successes and challenges. Besides reviewing business plans and financial projections, Afton conducted site visits, provided professional development, and attended strategic work sessions to gain a comprehensive understanding of educational and infrastructure resources needed to implement these school models successfully.

We've learned a lot. Schools and districts are investing in mobile devices and software, of course, but most say their most effective investments have been in engaging, developing, and supporting teachers and other staff to lead transformed classrooms. Indeed, investing in effective human capital may be the most important decision in sustaining technology-enabled school models.

As shown in Figure 7.1, of expenditures directly associated with starting and sustaining a cohort of tech-enabled school models, districts spent over 50% on "people" costs—namely, personnel and professional development. This may surprise those who tend to first think of the device, software, Wi-Fi, or something else that might require a plug or vast amounts of coding. Of these investments in people, positions include blended-learning coaches and technology specialists, while professional development has included consulting services, planning time, and site visits.

Professional development goes beyond traditional training activities; it also can include time for teacher planning and collaboration, and the cost of substitutes to allow for this flex time to occur. These changes may seem subtle from a budgetary perspective, but the time needed is significant. We

Figure 7.1. Financial Investment Areas in Technology-Enabled School Models

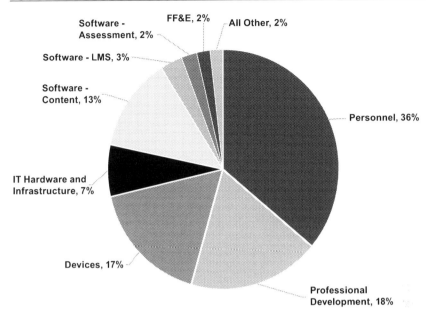

Note: These data reflect schools' and districts' projected 5-year expenditures associated with implementation of technology-enabled school models. The data represent the resource allocation plans for 11 districts, 110 schools, 850 classrooms, and 36,000 students as of fiscal year 2019.

have found this investment to be valuable, not only for developing teachers and staff, but also because it sends a clear message that this transformation is serious and teacher expertise is valued.

While people costs lead the pack in terms of expenditures, actual technology investments closely follow, at 42% of total costs—including devices, IT hardware and infrastructure, and software. Best practice districts began with a needs assessment to create an overall device strategy, including the type and number of devices, as well as grade configurations utilizing the hardware.

A basic needs assessment will answer several critical questions: What are the goals and objectives for technology-enabled classrooms for each grade? What type of technology can and should be leveraged to meet those goals? If devices are required, what type of devices and how will they be used—one for each student, a cart for the class, or something else? What type of content is required by subject area, and how will the district determine the most effective content to leverage? How will it measure success and iterate in future years?

Sites should perform needs assessments beginning on the classroom level and build a plan that allows for flexibility and assumes iterations based on lessons learned over time. This includes device breakage and refresh, but also the likelihood that content providers will change, or the mix of paid and free services provided will ebb and flow, as well as the possibility of new tools that will be developed and adopted over time. The needs assessment is a comprehensive process to link resource requirements to the goals and objectives of implementing a technology-enabled school model; it also will require annual iterations to reflect actual versus projected spending, and updated forecasts for future years.

While devices and other hardware are important, they are effective only with content and assessment tools that support the instructional vision. Our analysis found that districts planned to spend 16% of total investments on software, including 11% on content and 5% on "learning management systems," which, among other useful applications, can help track student performance. Much of that spending is on user licenses, which include both content and assessment tools. Yet study (Wood, 2018) after study (Davis, 2019) have shown an inefficient use of software licenses by school districts. As we will explain in more detail below, we recommend that leaders perform a thorough evaluation of software license use to identify funds that can be reallocated to other, more impactful investments, including effective professional development, engaging content, and even additional staff.

It's important not to be inflexible. Schools implementing technology need—and in our experience often have been given—the ability to "course-correct" during the year as they see fit. If a piece of software, an app, or a device was not deemed effective by the teacher, they often had the opportunity to change. While flexibility can be hard to build into school system operations, this approach seemed crucial to the success of many schools, allowing teachers to experiment to determine the most effective means to reach their kids. If these schools were "stuck" with the typical procurement cycle (i.e., commit resources for at least a full year), some of these models would not have been successful.

HOW DO SCHOOL SYSTEMS PAY FOR THIS?

Districts that have fared best in implementing technology-enabled models were given the time, space, and funding to allow for transformation to take place over time. They focused on building the right conditions, systems, and processes to support and sustain transformation. Most systems can create these conditions but may not have the luxury of significant added funding. They need to find other ways to afford technology-enabled school models. Here are a few strategies to consider.

Repurpose Nonpersonnel Funds

The most common source of funding in our experience is repurposed general funds, supplemented by federal and sometimes private grant dollars. Examples include purchasing technology with money previously used to purchase instructional materials and redeploying professional development budgets in ways that support the technology move.

This approach requires school or district leaders to systematically review, assess, and revise all major vendor contracts, with a focus on instructional materials and software licenses. The goal is to identify contract spending that does not align with the district's long-term vision and to highlight opportunities to renegotiate or cancel existing contracts.

Create a Strategic Staffing Plan

The typical district spends over 70% of its budget on staff, so several districts also performed a thorough review of their long-term staffing strategy to help fund positions that would support their future schools. To do this, a district can either (a) add new positions in place of those that are not essential for the future plan or (b) adjust roles and responsibilities of existing positions. Either strategy can have a significant impact on the fidelity of implementation of technology-enabled school models.

Several districts that we worked with undertook a position-by-position review of staff functions and identified several positions to modify or change over time—primarily through natural turnover—including those supporting school libraries, teachers' aides, and even operations support staff. The districts used the results to help fund new positions, while being intentional about leveraging turnover to help transform the district and schools over time.

This process of developing a long-term staffing plan, similar to the long-term technology plan we'll reference below, was an eye-opening process for district leadership. It was helpful to look at not only positions directly impacting the classroom, but also positions that might be a step removed, including assistant principals and librarians, as well as those in central office or districtwide positions. When a district envisions a fully implemented technology-enabled model, nearly all roles in the district will be impacted. This gives leadership an opportunity to proactively manage the inevitable turnover of school and central office positions to support the vision of the new pedagogic approach incorporating technology. This strategy also has the benefit of improving the chance for long-term sustainability, as the hiring process aligns with the ultimate goals and objectives of the initiative.

Establish a Device Fund

Best practices in device procurement include a thorough needs assessment by school, grade, and type of student to identify the types of devices required, when they will be needed, and any infrastructure changes that may be required. Thereafter, districts need to develop a detailed implementation plan, including how often devices will need to be "refreshed" or replaced, and how many to hold in inventory in case of loss or breakage (usually 5–10%). The device plan then leads to the funding plan.

Districts that we have worked with typically have invested a combination of existing general funds (usually earmarked for information technology), philanthropic or grant funds, and bond funds. Although best practice dictates maximizing the use of recurring general fund dollars, schools also may leverage bonding capacity. If they choose this path, the payback on those bonds should align directly with the life cycle of the devices being purchased; for example, if a device's useful life is 5 years, the amortization of bonds also should be over a 5-year period. Eventually, districts should consider building a "device fund" that could be drawn upon for ongoing adoptions and refreshes over time. One of the districts we worked with created an 8-year "technology long-range plan" that reflected the district's goals and objectives of technology implementation; the required investments in hardware, software, and devices to meet those goals; and an annual funding plan to support one-time and recurring investments in the plan. This district leveraged funds from a bond offering to spur the investments, then committed general funds to help refresh devices on an annual basis.

Other funding strategies that we have seen work well include leveraging existing or new partnerships, such as with local businesses or colleges, for in-kind services or program sharing; more strategic use of federal sources, such as Titles IA, II, and IVA funds; and ensuring strategic alignment between uses of all funding sources (sometimes referred to as "braiding funds") to eliminate duplicative or misaligned uses of dollars.

District structures, policies, and practices also may need to change in order to create the conditions for long-term success. What is the role of the finance department under this new academic paradigm? How do budgeting and planning practices change when information technology becomes a dominant learning medium? How should business operations change to support new operating models? And what are the implications of technology-enabled innovative learning models for financial governance?

When the education model changes dramatically, it's vital to configure all aspects of financial management and policy to support it so that the desired changes in schools can be effectively implemented and sustained at a quality level for years to come.

FIVE CRUCIAL PRACTICES THAT HAVE ENABLED THE EFFECTIVE IMPLEMENTATION OF INNOVATIVE SCHOOL MODELS

Align Academic and Financial Goals From the Start

Innovative academic plans should clearly articulate a vision for the future, with specific goals and measurable outcomes (for example, "implementing this bold new approach will improve 8th-grade math proficiency scores by 20% in 5 years"). Yet many schools and districts are stuck in an annual budget cycle that tends to overlook multiyear financial sustainability. A common misconception in the early stages of developing technology-enabled school models is that the pilot is too small, or the timing is too early, to contemplate financial sustainability. However, this is exactly the time for school teams to begin considering how their initiative can be financially sustained in the long term. Thinking about financial sustainability early allows a feedback loop from financial plans back into academic planning. In a world of limited resources, having clearly articulated academic goals, with an aligned resourcing and expenditure plan in place, can prevent a technology initiative from being cut for lack of funding. It provides transparency to all stakeholders on the needed resources and spurs critical conversations around return on investment and funding priorities.

Create a Detailed Long-Term Plan

Moving to a technology-enabled school model is not a one-time thing. It requires time to plan, procure, train, and implement. It calls for effective and recurrent professional development. Technology will require eventual refreshing. Instructional models will evolve, and with them the staffing, professional development, technology, and facility needs, all of which call for continued investment. That, in turn, calls for a long view of financial planning. Having such a view of expected needs will give a district time to plan for and secure funding sources (including spending trade-offs), identify long-lead resource requirements (such as infrastructure updates), and create a strong connection between the instructional model and capital-planning cycles. Long-term plans also can solicit stakeholder feedback and build buy-in and support (and in many instances, demand). In the process of developing the academic plan, a financial plan will help determine what's affordable and will inform implementation planning. When a classroom pilot is being implemented, the financial plan will guide decisions that ultimately will impact the entire school. And after the launch of a technology-enabled model, tracking actual results allows for variance analysis, reflects resource allocation changes, allows for comparison with other schools, and serves as a blueprint for scaling a successful model.

One of the most crucial factors in successful financial planning is the school leader's ability to discern what has made or will make the model successful, and then to ensure budgetary decisions that protect and promote those elements. These "key design elements" may include aspects of the model that define the teaching and learning approach, such as project-based learning or data-driven instruction. Because every initiative is different, it is fundamental that school principals be able to discern for themselves (or have the support to help them identify) what makes their school's instructional model work, understand the budgetary and financial policy levers at their disposal, and then align financial investments—both one-time and recurring—accordingly.

Another critical factor to the effectiveness of a financial plan is school-level ownership. Instructional strategy often is developed at the district level, but in many technology-enabled models, it is more localized. A personalization-of-instruction model ultimately requires ownership at the most local and personal level. The most successful models are owned by principals and classroom teachers. Ownership over implementation also includes responsibility for planning. Ownership over instructional planning is one change; ownership over resource planning (people, time, money, and space) is another change. Connecting the two is vital to the effective implementation of the most common technology-enabled models. For a truly innovative model to be fully implemented, a principal likely will require different kinds of staffing and nonpersonnel supports than in the past. Can principals set hiring criteria based on the unique needs of their school model? Could, for example, the librarian position responsibilities evolve to support a technology resource lab? Could centralized textbook money be used instead for teacher-determined digital content needs? Could centrally organized professional development be replaced with school-specific teacher planning and collaboration time or site visits? Could school principals influence the kinds of teacher experience and skill sets that the HR department uses to screen candidates? These and other questions need to be considered as potential policy and practice changes are considered and implemented that will likely shift the locus of control from central to school level.

Identify Potential Challenges and Eliminate Them

Once long-term financial and implementation plans have been developed, schools and districts may identify certain policy constraints that could interfere with those plans. Common examples are class-size limits, contractual agreements, and procurement policies. Willingness to tackle such challenges is crucial for successful implementation of a major innovation like this. Sometimes, however, constraints are only perceived—not real. When things have been done a certain way for a long time, it may be assumed that this is due to a particular constraint, such as contractual language. In reality, this may just be common practice. Therefore, it is important to drill down to the root cause of challenges in order to find solutions. Even in the case where constraints are real, it is important to consider long-term options to resolve them.

School models using technology come in all shapes and sizes. Some utilize small groups with different learning modalities. Others have many students using devices, with teachers and other staff monitoring data and facilitating personalized learning sequences and with coaching provided as needed. But many districts and states have policies that restrict classes from exceeding certain limits. These policies need to be revisited, especially considering that the "classroom," when it incorporates technology-enabled personalized learning environments, is not necessarily the same as it used to be. For example, one school we worked with repurposed an electives-teacher position to a personalized-learning-coach position. To do this, class sizes were increased via waivers beyond district policy, and instructional support staff were deployed to assist teachers with increased class sizes. Notably, this plan was developed *with* the impacted teaching staff—a critical factor to the model's success. As its instructional strategy was transformed, the full school benefited from the personalized learning coach. With resources tight, this could not have been accomplished without the ability to exceed class-size maximums. While we don't recommend large classes in general (and do not consider technology to be a replacement for effective instruction), policies that don't allow flexibility, even when supported by school leadership, can be a barrier to innovation.

Technology-enabled school models often require specific equipment, instructional materials, professional development for teachers, and even furniture. Some school needs may fall outside a district's purchase order process and list of approved vendors. When a school's needs for technology differ from what the district's IT department typically supports, this becomes even more complicated. The district and its schools must balance their shared innovation goals with efficiency and effective controls. Procurement has been reported to us as the biggest challenge principals face in attempting to innovate in their schools' instructional model. As one principal explained, his team spent more than 8 months trying to get out-of-spec furniture approved by central office procurement. Districts considering innovation must be willing to take a critical eye to procurement in light of changing school needs. By revisiting class-size and procurement policies in response to the changing school model, district leaders can move toward being enablers—rather than roadblocks—to innovation.

Understand Where Trade-Offs May Exist, Particularly in the Long Term

Also crucial for implementation success is a willingness to evaluate potential resource allocation changes, a.k.a. "trade-offs." One example that's often seen in technology-enabled school models is to reduce spending on textbooks and increase spending on digital content. Sometimes, however, trade-off choices aren't visible in financial statements because they deal more with reprioritizations of effort or focus within existing resources. For example, devices already in the school may no longer be used in a computer lab and instead be used in classrooms. Other examples are to reduce administrative staffing in order to afford extended-day pay for teachers and to adjust staffing priorities to free up a teaching position. As noted above, one school used existing non-instructional positions to increase class sizes in electives, freeing up a teacher to become an instructional coach. In these scenarios, position counts or total salaries did not change, but the use of positions changed substantially.

The above examples are relatively small trade-offs meant to foster innovation at one school. When a full system is moving toward innovative school models, trade-offs may include evaluating central office staffing and expenditures in order to reallocate resources to the school level.

Manage and Measure Outcomes

Few school systems have been in the habit of budgeting and reporting spending at the school level, although this is beginning to change under ESSA due to the financial transparency provision that requires states to publish school-level spending data. This lack of school-specific reporting transparency created an inherent historical challenge in determining the financial implications of a school's instructional model. Reporting and tracking spending at the building level allows for an understanding of the resource allocation decisions that stem from a technology-enabled learning model, while tabulating the cost of the model. This crucial practice ensures that the district understands what is being spent at each school and can evaluate the return on that investment by examining the school's academic outcomes. This enables the district to prioritize investment and investigate potential best practices that are ripe for replication.

In sum, when moving toward technology-enabled school models, districts should consider financial sustainability. Practices that strengthen that financial sustainability over time include developing long-range financial plans aligned with key design elements, evaluating and loosening policies that restrict innovation, ensuring that schools have support when making trade-offs, and tracking spending and monitoring against the plan.

RECOMMENDATIONS FOR THE FIELD

While schools should lead development of instructional and financial sustainability plans for their pilots and full-scale models, districts have a key role to play in creating the financial conditions that allow innovation to flourish and grow to scale. Districts must align their financial systems, structures, policies, and practices with their changing instructional strategy. They also must equip school leaders with the requisite training and support, as financial planning may be new to many principals. In this way, schools can implement technology-enabled innovation with the help, rather than in spite, of the district. Funders—federal, state, local, and private—can play an important role in this work by ensuring funding flexibility and creating incentives for these financial best practices within districts.

If academic innovation is to boost student outcomes across a district, the district will want to be prepared to expand it into other grades and other schools. To prepare for scaling up such innovative academic models, it is essential that academic, finance, operations, and technology teams work together in developing long-range plans. The lead time required for policy changes, system enhancements, and capital improvements can be lengthy, but academic innovation is unfolding rapidly.

Based on our experience, we can offer these recommendations.

For School Leaders

Understand your school's existing spending plan as a whole, including all staff and how time and scheduling impact spending. Draw the connections between your school's priorities and goals and the resource allocation decisions that are inherent in your budget. Ensure that you know what key design elements make your school's technology-enabled plan work, and see that they have priority in spending decisions. Ask questions of and ask for partnership from your district finance team. Think outside the box in your planning, and question any financial policies and practices that you may see as obstacles to your ideal planning. Raise your voice when roadblocks or hurdles arise, and find your advocate at the central office to help you forge an innovation path at your district in the short term, while systems and structures are changed for the long term.

For District Finance Teams and Leaders

Focus on long-term planning and the conditions necessary for success. If your district presently does not plan beyond the current budget cycle, consider developing a long-range "base case" plan. Run parallel paths of school-level planning for pilots and district-level planning for transformation. Identify a point person to help innovative school leaders navigate the system and act as their advocate. Ensure that school leaders have the capacity to take on resource-planning ownership through professional development and protection of school leader and teacher time. Ask what you can stop doing, and ensure genuine two-way communication channels.

For the "System"

Find ways to create flexibility in funding sources. Ensure that technology-enabled school models aren't just about the devices. Free up burdensome restrictions and avoid increasing requirements. Trust school and classroom leaders and empower them to be innovators through policy.

Financial planning for technology-enabled school models is essential for sustainability and scaling. School leaders and teachers are best positioned to develop and own these models. The best-laid plans are unlikely to succeed without the conditions necessary for success. Our belief, based on early successes in the field, is that schools with a supportive central office culture will be the most successful in this work.

REFERENCES

Davis, M. R. (2019, May 14). *K–12 districts wasting millions by not using purchased software, new analysis finds.* marketbrief.edweek.org/marketplace-k-12 /unused-educational-software-major-source-wasted-k-12-spending-new-analysis -finds

Futuresource Consulting. (n.d.). *K–12 education market continues to provide growth opportunities.* www.futuresource-consulting.com/press-release/education-techno logy-press/k-12-education-market-continues-to-provide-growth-opportunities -to-pc-oems-and-the-major-os-providers

Wood, C. (2018, November 9). *Most educational software licenses go unused in K–12 districts.* edscoop.com/most-educational-software-licenses-arent-used-in -k-12-districts

CHAPTER 8

Breaking the Vise of Declining Enrollment

Karen Hawley Miles

To the average parent or community member, student enrollment decline may seem worrisome yet potentially positive. After all, with fewer students in the same facilities, shouldn't there be smaller classes and more resources to go around? But as any school system leader can attest, declining enrollment in fact creates a vise that, if unaddressed, can erode quality and squeeze out innovation and needed investment. This is because with every lost pupil, revenue declines while per-pupil costs rise. Class sizes do drop—but not necessarily in ways that help students.

Many districts focus on simply reducing costs, perhaps through closing schools or finding a short-term infusion of cash. But there is a more strategic approach. Cost pressure creates an opportunity to revisit the ways that people, time, technology, and money are organized, drawing lessons from high-performing schools and districts. This fundamental shift requires involving the community in creating a shared vision, as well as changing longstanding mindsets, contracts, and regulations. District and school leaders need to collaborate with a broad set of stakeholders to make this transformation effective and sustainable.

This chapter describes the financial impact of declining enrollment and then outlines five strategies for stakeholders to consider that have the potential to turn the challenge into an opportunity for restructuring resources in ways that accelerate school performance. School systems can be successful at any size, as long as they are strategically designed to ensure that every student can access a strong school.

UNDERSTANDING THE VISE: THE FINANCIAL IMPACT OF DECLINING ENROLLMENT

Nationwide, total public school enrollment has been mostly increasing since the 1950s, except for a few dips (U.S. Department of Education, 2017). Yet declining enrollment remains a significant concern, particularly for large urban and any type of small districts. About one-quarter of large urban districts (those with more than 20,000 students) and slightly more than half of small districts (with 10,000 or fewer students, whether rural, urban, or suburban) lost more than 5% of their enrollment between 2006 and 2016.[1] The median large urban district lost 10%, but some cities—including Milwaukee, Washington, DC, Philadelphia, St. Louis, Pittsburgh, and Cleveland—lost 15 to 30% (U.S. Department of Education, n.d.). The median small district lost an average of 22% of enrollment. By 2028, the National Center for Education Statistics projects enrollment to decrease in 22 states, many of which are more likely to have small districts (U.S. Department of Education, 2019).

Enrollment drops for many reasons, including declining birth rates, decreased immigration, and economic mobility, as families move around in search of jobs or different climates (McBride et al., 2013; Rich, 2012; Warren, 2019). Particularly in urban districts, many families also may choose charter, private, or parochial schools, or home schooling. For example, from 1999 to 2016, enrollment in traditional New York City public schools dropped by about the same amount as charter enrollment grew.[2] Rural areas have been particularly hard-hit by cutbacks in coal mining, agriculture, and manufacturing (Truong, 2018). District leaders need to unpack the specific drivers of enrollment in their area to understand whether decline will continue, which grade levels it will affect and when, and whether there might be ways to stem the tide.

Revenue Drops With Each Lost Student

Regardless of the reason for the exit, each student who leaves a district takes dollars with them. To get an estimate of how much, first we must consider that, on average, district revenue comes 42% from local, 50% from state, and 8% from federal sources (U.S. Census Bureau, 2019). Local funds usually are based on property taxes and thus don't change immediately with enrollment (although persistent population decline eventually will reduce the tax base). On the other hand, most state and federal funds are attached to enrollment or attendance, although the formulas can be complex.

Roughly speaking, then, if a district spends the national average of $12,200 per pupil, when one student leaves, the district could lose up to 58%—or $7,067—from state and federal revenue (U.S. Census Bureau, 2019). When 10 leave, this totals $70,670, or about what it costs to pay the average teacher salary plus benefits.

Of course, this estimate changes significantly based on the state funding model. First, the portion of revenue coming from state and federal sources varies widely, from a low of 36% in New Hampshire to a high of 93% in neighboring Vermont or 80% in New Mexico (U.S. Census Bureau, 2019).

Districts in states that rely more on local and less on state and federal funds will have more stable revenues as enrollments decline. Second, states have different rules for how funds move from districts to charters. Some states, like Texas, require districts to shift virtually the entire per-pupil spending amount to the receiving charter school, including all revenue sources; others, like Indiana and Maine, do not. Some states fund a transition period before the full amount must be shifted ("FundEd: Charters," 2020). And of course, states vary widely in their average per-pupil allocation, from about $7,000 to $23,000 (U.S. Census Bureau, 2019).

Spending Doesn't Drop as Quickly or as Much as Enrollment

While revenue drops with each lost student, most costs stay the same. This happens because the vast majority of district spending pays for staff positions—and districts cannot reduce the teaching workforce in proportion to enrollment. For example, if the aforementioned 10 students are scattered across grades within a school, as they usually are—three from 3rd grade, two from 5th grade, etc.—the school still needs the same number of teachers. Additionally, union contracts, state regulations, and city politics often make it difficult to reduce personnel or adopt other strategies that might enable lower, more easily adjustable spending—like contracting out services or staff.

But there are several factors at play. At Education Resource Strategies, the nonprofit I lead, we have partnered with or studied over 100 school systems since 2005 and have developed a detailed database of budget information from 25 urban districts, ranging in size from 20,000 to 500,000 students (see Table 8.1). Drawing on these data, we can understand how cost dynamics play out in various ways.

Let's begin by understanding the district budget. Typically, districts spend about:

- *77% of dollars on staff salaries and benefits, materials, and services located in schools.* This includes teachers, principals, aides, and secretaries, as well as people who might be reported on central office budgets but who actually work in schools, like instructional coaches, custodians, and social workers.
- *15% on what we call "shared services."* This includes transportation, food, and facilities maintenance that play out in schools but are budgeted centrally.
- *8% on district office overhead or "leadership and management."* This category includes the superintendent, that individual's cabinet, administrators such as the facilities director and director of transportation, and principal supervisors. It also includes functions that are district-level responsibilities, such as legal services, payroll, and human resources.

Table 8.1. Average Urban District Spending by Category

Spending Category	% Budget	Often budgeted centrally	Often considered for contracting
Central office	22.8%		
Leadership and management	7.6%		
Business services (data processing, finance, legal, insurance)	2.4%	X	X
Special population program management and support	0.7%	X	
Human resources	0.6%	X	X
Governance	0.5%	X	
Curriculum development	0.4%	X	X
All other leadership and management (~20 functions)	3.0%	X	
Shared services	15.2%		
Food services	5.0%	X	X
Transportation	4.8%	X	X
Facilities and maintenance	2.1%	X	X
All other (various itinerant positions across departments)	3.3%	X	
School level	77.2%		
Classroom staff	*48.1%*		
Teachers	42.7%		
Teacher aides	4.6%		
Substitutes	0.8%	X	
School leadership and operations	*10.4%*		
Principals	1.8%		
Vice principals	1.8%		
Instructional coaches	1.5%	X	X
Custodians	2.4%	X	X
Secretaries/clerks/other administrative personnel	1.9%		
Coordinator/manager	1.0%	X	
Student support	*8.1%*		

Table 8.1. Average Urban District Spending by Category (continued)

Spending Category	% Budget	Often budgeted centrally	Often considered for contracting
Guidance counselors	1.4%	X	
Speech therapists	0.8%	X	
Social workers	0.7%		
Librarians	0.7%		
School monitors/security	0.7%	X	
Psychologists	0.6%	X	
Nurses	0.5%	X	
All other positions	2.7%		
Nonpersonnel	*10.6%*		
Instructional materials and supplies	3.0%		
Noninstructional supplies/services	1.0%		
Utilities	2.3%		
Other	4.3%		

Note: ERS analysis of 25 urban districts ranging in size from 20,000 to 500,000.

Let's focus first on leadership and management costs, which range from 6 to 10% of total spending. This covers systemwide roles and contracts, which may be difficult to remove or reduce. Even with a decline of a few hundred students, the accounting department must still operate. If a district is at the highest end of leadership and management spending, it might be possible to free up 4% of the budget by finding efficiencies or making hard trade-offs about what can be accomplished reasonably—but even this won't be enough in the context of a 10% enrollment decline.

Next, let's explore shared services. The largest components of that category are student transportation, food services, and facilities maintenance. By and large, these operations are not structured so that costs can be adjusted readily according to demand. For example, transporting 10 fewer students likely won't eliminate a bus route or change the need to fix a roof. If the district provides cafeteria services, even food service costs don't go down much because so much of the cost is labor. Most services are staffed by full-time staff members who may be protected by contract or state statute from layoff or have options to fill other district jobs—even if those jobs don't fit their background.

Finally, let's explore the main cost drivers at the school level. As Table 8.1 shows, the majority of school spending pays for teachers, leaders, and support staff. Especially in the beginning, enrollment usually declines gradually across grades or in cohorts of students based on birth rates, but is not necessarily concentrated in one specific school or classroom. As noted above, when just a few students leave from each class, schools cannot reduce teachers. Similarly, a drop in students doesn't mean that the school can operate without a principal, librarian, or guidance counselor. Most districts' union contracts don't allow part-time or contract positions in schools, although of course they could, and some spread one staff member across several schools.

Even if it was possible to reduce personnel at the school or central office level, several factors make that difficult to do. The school district may be one of the largest employers in the city, and reducing personnel has a ripple effect on the city economy and the community, even on parents who may be employees. Contracts, state regulations, and accreditation standards sometimes make it hard to reduce personnel effectively. For example, many contracts and states require that both teaching and nonteaching personnel be laid off in order of seniority regardless of their performance, expertise, or specific role. These realities shouldn't preclude downsizing where necessary, but rather underscore the need for political courage, leadership stability, and wide community involvement to devise the most effective solutions and remove barriers to flexible, more strategic use of resources.

Cost per Student Sometimes Rises With Declining Enrollment

Making the situation even trickier, two factors actually raise the underlying cost per student. First, enrollment decline sometimes results in a concentration of needier students, as parents with more financial resources move to surrounding suburbs, or the highest-achieving young graduates leave rural districts for jobs (Center on Reinventing Public Education, 2017; Owens et al., 2016; Rich, 2012). For example, in Philadelphia, enrollment declined 18% from 2008 to 2015, while the percentage of students requiring special education services went from 14% to 18%. If students move to charter schools, this also may leave behind a higher concentration of students who need special education services or academic remediation. A 2017 analysis by ERS found that 12% of Oakland Unified School District (OUSD) students needed special education services, compared with 7% in Oakland charters, and incoming 6th- and 9th-graders in OUSD were less likely to be academically proficient than their peers in charter schools (Education Resource Strategies & Oakland Achieves, 2017). This intensification of student need created financial challenges for both OUSD and the School District of Philadelphia because both California and Pennsylvania reimbursed the district at much less than the cost of serving students with special education needs, not to mention those requiring the most intensive services.

Second, the average cost of teacher compensation often rises in districts with declining enrollment. More experienced teachers earn more in salary and benefits (like family health plans and pension payments) than the most junior teachers—sometimes as much as two times more (Miles et al., 2015). As a district loses enrollment, it usually stops hiring and may even lay off teachers. Union contracts and state-level due-process regulations typically require that districts reduce staff in a "last in, first out" model. Over a few years, this pushes average compensation costs up. For example, the Cleveland Metropolitan School District (CMSD) lost 44% of enrollment from 2002 to 2012; by the end of that time period, 92% of teachers had worked in the district for more than 8 years and half for more than 15 years. The average compensation of these teachers was over $100,000. We will explore later in this chapter how CMSD tackled this by directly addressing the contract provisions that had the perverse effect of protecting some teachers who were not delivering for students.

WHAT CAN DISTRICT AND SCHOOL LEADERS DO?

District communities can employ five strategies to tackle these challenges. These strategies share three features. First, they begin with a strategic vision for what needs to happen in schools to accelerate learning for every child. Second, they use the disruption of declining enrollment to shift resources, as well as processes, timelines, and accountability in support of this vision. Third, they aim to use resources efficiently—defined as attaining the most crucial student or service outcomes at the lowest possible cost. The five strategies include:

1. Reinvent the district office while actively managing costs
2. Create flexibility and capacity to redesign schools to accelerate learning and transform the teaching job
3. Transform the portfolio of schools by closing or reconfiguring schools
4. Manage the workforce and redesign compensation
5. Explore ways to increase revenue

Reinvent the District Office While Actively Managing Costs

Budget pressure always generates a call to reduce district office spending because it doesn't immediately impact the classroom. This often leads to such stopgap measures as freezing hiring, drawing down reserves, or deferring maintenance.

These steps sometimes may be necessary, but only in the short term while district leaders organize the community to craft a more sustainable strategy. Cost pressure presents an opportunity to reenvision the district office role and focus district-level spending on a few powerful improvement strategies, including clarifying how the district office can better support schools and streamline services. Districts can start by addressing three questions:

- Where can the district find efficiencies?
- Are there opportunities to lower costs or make them more variable using contracted services or part-time roles without compromising quality?
- What resources and decisions might district leaders devolve from central to school level to foster stewardship and better match spending to school-specific needs?

Finding Efficiencies. If district leaders undertake a rigorous, open-minded study—for example, by comparing spending levels by function and analyzing service quality—they often can find pockets of overspending or low return on investment. Districts then will want to ask whether high spending is strategic or the result of outmoded policies or inefficiencies that could be addressed with technology and information systems.

Boston Public Schools (BPS) presents an interesting example. In 2015, after years of declining enrollment and annual budget cuts, Chief Financial Officer Eleanor Laurans and her team undertook a thorough spending review with support from ERS, which clearly identified the reasons for the deficit. The leadership team then convened a Long-Term Financial Planning Committee that included community advocates, the school committee president, the union president, and others.

This group identified "10 big ideas" for addressing the deficit, which included restructuring teacher compensation while increasing student time, changing the school portfolio, and addressing extremely high transportation spending (Boston Public Schools, 2016). BPS found that it cost $1,500 per pupil per year on average for bus services (ranging from $400 to a whopping $5,000), compared with an average of $300 per pupil across the 200 largest districts. District leaders implemented a host of innovative practices that are bringing spending down, including encouraging public transit options for 7th- and 8th-graders and high school students, actively promoting the idea of "opting out" of bus transportation, and hosting a "hackathon" that challenged teams from across the country to develop cheaper, better-quality bus routing systems (Baskin, 2017; Johnson, 2017).

Districts often can find efficiencies by analyzing how many staff they have at each position level. When enrollment drops, districts often cut junior staff members first, leaving each department leader with as few as one to three staff members instead of the six to 10 direct reports we might see in other organizations (Neilson & Wulf, 2012; Bandiera et al., 2014). Instead, districts can perform a "span of control" analysis to make sure that teams remain well-balanced even after cuts. In one district that ERS studied, the district office comprised 24 teams with zero to two individual contributors for every manager or director. Over time these small, top-heavy teams became siloed even when they worked in related areas (e.g., talent, accounting, and payroll). To address this, the district reorganized to rebalance spans of control, break down silos, and create more collaborative school support.

Districts often end up with relatively high central office spending toward the middle of their enrollment decline, and that is where an efficiency review can be most helpful. But after years of annual central office cuts, cutting further can create extreme dysfunction (Education Resource Strategies, 2015; Kelley, 2015). Districts must strive for return on investment—and sometimes cutting services does not provide a meaningful return. At this point, district leaders need to consider other reorganization and redesign strategies.

Contracting Services Out. Enrollment decline offers an opportunity to improve service quality and make costs more variable by contracting with providers that have greater scale and expertise. This can be in the larger spending areas, like transportation, food services, and business services, or in areas less often considered for contracting out, like recruiting, professional development, and curriculum development. These criteria can help guide decisionmaking:

- Is the service critical to the district's theory of action for how to improve and support schools?
- Is the current service model meeting its goals, and do "customers"—schools, teachers, or parents—rate it highly?
- Can the district provide the service at a cost comparable to similar districts?
- Can the district vary the cost of service delivery just as easily as an outside provider if enrollment changes?

If the answer to any of these questions is "no," then stakeholders might consider whether engaging with an outside contractor or partner makes sense. For example, in 2015, principals in Baltimore City Schools reported low satisfaction with the bookkeeping and finance support provided by the district business services office. To increase accountability, reduce costs, and improve usefulness, the district put those dollars into school budgets and created relationships with two different private companies that principals could choose from *if* they wanted these services.

Devolving Resources and Decisionmaking to Schools. Finally, district leaders also might consider giving principals more flexibility over their resource use. This can enable school leaders to make the trade-offs that meet their school's unique needs, rather than just dealing with the impact of across-the-board cuts. When coupled with a revisioning of the central role in providing support, this can create a more "customer"-service-oriented approach. In 2013, CMSD engaged a team of district, community, and school leaders to evaluate resource allocation and push as many resources as possible to the school level (Cleveland Metropolitan School District, n.d.; Travers & Hitchcock, 2015). This made sense because the district simultaneously was implementing a plan to give schools more autonomy and support; therefore, the district retained services that were central to district strategy, were high-compliance or high-risk, or benefited from economies of scale (such as principal recruiting, school police services, building repair, legal services, and transportation).

After implementing this approach for the 2014–2015 school year, the district moved the percentage of the budget over which school leaders had discretion from 2% to 71% (Education Resource Strategies, n.d.). Table 8.1 shows the categories of spending that districts sometimes hold centrally that they might devolve if they were seeking to maximize school-level discretion in areas such as student support services, which include guidance counselors, psychologists, social workers, and more. Devolving professional development resources also can make sense when schools are implementing widely varying programs or have big differences in teacher and leadership capacity.

In the following years, Cleveland's central office leaders reenvisioned themselves as "service providers," creating service agreements with schools related to services that the schools now "purchase" from the central office, and offering bundled packages that match particular school strategies. For example, schools implementing Montessori academic designs can purchase a customized set of supports, including professional development and curricular materials.

Some school systems, such as Denver, Boston, and Lawrence, MA, have gone even further by creating a portfolio with a range of governance structures, including charters, innovation schools, or pilot schools alongside more traditional schools. This provides even more opportunities to tailor resources to school needs. Devolving resources in a way that actually results in better use of resources requires that principals have the capacity to rethink school organization, as well as flexibility from a host of district and sometimes state constraints and contracts, which we discuss in more detail below.

Create the Flexibility and Build Capacity to Redesign Schools

Schools that dramatically accelerate student performance often "do school" differently than the traditional classroom and scheduling models that have dominated education for the past 50 years (Miles & Frank, 2008). Table 8.2. outlines the critical shifts that these schools make.

Table 8.2. School Design Shifts

Design Essential	From		To
Teacher Collaboration	Teaching as an individual enterprise	→	Teams of teachers who work together to execute a collective vision for excellent instruction and their own professional improvement
	A "one-size-fits-all" teaching job	→	Roles and assignments that match each individual's unique skills and expertise to needed roles
Personalized Time and Attention	Standardized class sizes in "one-teacher classrooms"	→	Groups of teachers and students that vary across subjects, activities, and students
	Rigid time allocations	→	Flexible schedules that allow time to vary with needs of students
Whole Child	Investments in culture and social–emotional support that remove resources from core instruction	→	Investments that are embedded within and reinforce the school's core instructional work

Enacting these shifts requires disrupting traditional ways of organizing people, time, and money in five key ways:

- Shifting teachers to core subjects and early grades to lower teacher load and enable small-group and individual instruction
- Reassigning teachers to leverage expertise and enable deliberate teaming
- Rethinking school schedules to vary and expand time for students and enable time for teacher teaming
- Leveraging technology and community partnerships to expand program offerings and after-school opportunities
- Exploring part-time or contracted roles for noninstructional and noncore offerings

Disruptions like declining enrollment provide an opportunity to examine old practices, lower costs, and move in new directions. For example, high schools we've worked with have reimagined how to offer very small elective courses more cost-effectively through online or remote instructional strategies, early college credits at community colleges, or partnerships with community or nonprofit organizations. Cost pressure also can generate openness to creating part-time working arrangements or job-sharing. These types of strategies can free up enough resources to invest more in priority areas like teacher leadership, time for collaboration, and lowering teacher load in early-grade core subjects like literacy and numeracy.

These new school designs cannot be enacted by individual school leaders alone. Making these changes requires changing the people in schools, creating new schedules, using staff and time differently, and using new arrangements. Principals and leaders need support in order to envision new ways of organizing, and in many cases contractual clauses and state regulations will need to be changed to create flexibilities in five areas:

- Allow position reductions. Given the need to honor job protections, this may require transition funding from districts and states as schools undertake staffing changes.
- Remove across-the-board, class-size maximums so that school leaders can be strategic about providing students with periods of individual attention balanced with larger group sizes, thereby maximizing the impact of the most effective teachers.
- Enable more flexibility in instructor-of-record policies so school leaders can leverage untraditional providers, such as paraprofessionals and resident teachers.
- Enable partnerships with community service providers so that school leaders can take advantage of the wealth of talent in the community to provide cost-effective and high-quality staffing solutions for special subject classes or other purposes.
- Remove strict guidelines around daily use of and amount of teacher and student time.

Transform the Portfolio of Schools by Closing and/or Reconfiguring Schools

After significant enrollment decline, districts find themselves operating schools that are much smaller than planned. Underutilized, subscale schools drive the largest per-pupil cost increases. Subscale schools organized in traditional ways cost more both because they spread the fixed cost of administration and building operation over fewer students and because schools cannot simply eliminate one position when a handful of students leave across classrooms. While small schools offer benefits, often including smaller classes and the potential for a more tight-knit school community, maintaining an unintentionally small school can make it hard to cost-effectively offer art, music, and physical education, or a diverse array of electives at the secondary level. In addition, schools with small numbers of students per grade will have a difficult time implementing the research-backed strategies described above.

ERS defines a "subscale school" as one that is filled at 85% capacity or below, or has only one or two classrooms per grade or secondary-level subject. This translates to roughly 350 students for elementary schools and 500 or fewer for K–8 schools and secondary schools. Within the database of districts we've studied, ERS has found that districts spend about 20% more per pupil (ranging from 12 to 25%) in these small schools.

Moreover, high-spending, underutilized schools often serve high concentrations of economically disadvantaged students. These students often need more support—but the extra spending doesn't go toward strategies that are likely to improve student outcomes. In our analysis, we found that only about one-third of the extra spending is driven by the cost of administration and building operations. Most of the additional spending pays for classrooms not filled to target levels– and this does not occur in predictable ways. In any given year, 1st-grade classes might happen to be much bigger than 5th-grade classes, even if it makes strategic sense to provide more individual support in 1st grade. And this is exacerbated in subscale secondary schools, where class sizes for electives are often much smaller than for foundational, core subjects.

Defining the design challenge as "small grade-level cohorts" rather than "small schools" can change the mindset and open up new considerations for the district portfolio. Rather than thinking first about which schools to close, the community can think about how they might change grade configurations and combine schools to enable better grade-level teacher teams; more opportunities for flexible, skill-based grouping; and concentration of specialized teacher expertise. In this new paradigm, a district might even think about how to leverage its most experienced school and teacher leaders, spreading them over two schools in a shared vertical path or across two school teams that share the same grade level.

For example, ERS worked with one low-funded Midwestern district that had numerous subscale schools caused by enrollment decline. Rethinking grade configuration offered an opportunity to reduce costs and improve student experience. In this district, students attended K–6 schools, followed by grades 7–12 schools. At the same time, magnets and most charter schools offered a middle school experience beginning at 6th grade—which meant that many students left their neighborhood schools after 5th grade. In a school with only two classrooms per grade, this pattern created a staffing and morale challenge, as schools had to either squeeze all the remaining students into one very large class or offer two very small classrooms. Sometimes the remaining students felt "left behind" when their classmates moved to new, possibly more exciting environments. To address these challenges, the district worked with the community to create fewer K–5 schools and move 6th-graders into a reenvisioned middle school model. In doing so, it created a more equitable experience for all students, closed a school that needed significant facilities work, and concentrated resources to enable a richer middle grades experience than most students had previously.

The possibilities offered by reconfiguration are many, but they are always context-specific. After years of declining enrollment, Holyoke, MA, has nine small schools serving students in grades pre-K–8 in various configurations. The community is in the process of closing two schools and moving to a consistent districtwide model for elementary and middle schools, as consolidating students into two midsized schools in the middle grades enables richer program offerings and student supports. At the same time, the creation of middle schools opens the opportunity for community-wide engagement in a visioning process to identify the student and teacher experience the district wants to create.

Manage Workforce and Revise Compensation Structure

Many districts that have experienced years of declining enrollment face at least one of two issues that drive up the underlying cost of education. First, the district may find itself with an increasingly senior workforce, due to hiring freezes and "last in, first out" layoffs. Average salaries and the cost of benefits like health care and pensions are inherently higher with a senior workforce. Second, virtually all districts provide automatic salary increases with years of experience, without linking increases to greater leadership responsibilities, teaching effectiveness, or expertise. This means that average salaries go up without changing anything about how the district can organize teachers or time. Teacher compensation could be structured to rise with experience, but, for example, some of the increase could be redirected to pay for teachers who take on more challenging roles that require greater leadership, more time, or more expertise. Such a restructuring actually can raise the maximum levels of salary that teachers can earn.

In 2012, Cleveland Metropolitan School District faced both of these challenges. With 92% of teachers having 8 or more years of experience, the average teacher salary had risen to $100,000 or more, and there were limited opportunities to bring in new energy or leverage experienced teachers to mentor the next generation. Acting upon the urgency created by a looming $64 million deficit, the district and union negotiated a new contract in 2013 that garnered 71% approval. This contract shifted dollars away from increases for experience and into paying teachers for taking on leadership roles, working in high-needs schools, and taking hard-to-staff positions. It also created more flexibility for using time in schools differently and requirements for collaborative-planning time that would allow teachers to grow in their craft. Importantly, it shifted hiring to the school level and moved away from staffing based solely on order of seniority to focus first on qualifications for the job, balanced with experience.

Next, the district employed three strategies to reinvigorate and rebalance its workforce. First, the district made a data-driven pitch to then-Governor John Kasich showing the financial impact of such a senior workforce. He granted $6 million to help the district offer an early retirement incentive, which the union helped to implement. To make the incentive as effective as possible, the union and district team reached out to teachers who might have wanted to leave the teaching force but were staying to achieve retirement plan eligibility, as well as to those who weren't actively engaged in improving instruction and student performance. At the same time, they reached out to high-performing experienced teachers to encourage them to remain. Second, the district invested in extra human resources staff to actively manage out 100 low-performing teachers. They focused first on an astonishingly large number of teachers who had been absent for 20 or more days—eight more than students can be absent in 1 year. Third, they retooled their recruiting efforts and new teacher onboarding strategies to raise the quality of new hires and keep them.

As a result of these efforts, by 2016 the Cleveland teaching workforce was much more balanced, with over a third of teachers in their first 7 years. In addition, average compensation dropped by $9,000 per teacher in inflation-adjusted dollars, resulting in $18 million more dollars to be spent elsewhere. Over the same period, the maximum salary teachers could earn in Cleveland went up to support expert teachers in new teacher-leader roles (Education Resource Strategies, n.d.). Such an inspiring story demonstrates the complex possibilities that exist for addressing a district's largest budget item in a way that works for teachers and students.

Explore Ways to Increase Revenue

Districts we've worked with employ two major strategies for increasing revenue: winning back enrollment and making the case to state and local officials for more funds. Winning enrollment from students who live in the region requires increasing quality over the long term, but three shorter-term tactics can pay off more quickly: offering unique programming, expanding pre-K, and creating new high school options.

For example, Massachusetts's Holyoke Public Schools (HPS) piloted in one elementary school a dual-language Spanish program that generated rave reviews and high demand. Despite limited resources, district leaders expanded that program to two schools and most grades, and the program now boasts a waiting list. At the same time, the district expanded its pre-K enrollment from 135 seats to 280, which represents about 3% of district enrollment. HPS also created better programs to recapture dropouts. These types of programs not only bring in revenue, but can open up opportunities for partnerships and potential cost savings. For example, districts can partner with community colleges or universities to offer dual credit, or with nonprofit organizations to offer a customized set of courses and experiences (S. Zrike, personal interview, July 12, 2019).

Making the case for more revenue in the context of extremely poor performance and years of deficits can be challenging because these conditions often erode public trust. To regain that trust, it's important for districts to transparently discuss the drivers of financial challenge, as well as potential solutions, with the wider community. Because children in schools bear the brunt of financial challenge, district leaders also need to leverage the pain of reduction and disruption that reinventing practice entails and focus scarce resources on doing a few priority things well.

The School District of Philadelphia (SDP) dramatically illustrates these strategies in action. From 2000 to 2012, the district lost about a quarter of its enrollment—50,000 students—and in 2012 faced a deficit of about $300 million.[3] It first tried to address the problem by closing 23 schools, but still needed to issue $300 million in debt to finance the next school year. In 2014, the district had to cut nearly 3,800 positions, leaving an empty central office and schools with almost no staff except teachers and principals (Karnash & Quinones, 2013; School District of Philadelphia, 2013).

Even as they were downsizing, district leaders continued to invest in improving outcomes. For example, the district chose not to close some of the underenrolled schools in areas of high poverty, but instead to convert them to in-district charter schools with much more flexibility to do things like expand hours, use time differently, and hire different staff. This strategy was required because the union would not work with the district to create the flexibilities that would enable such redesign. They also concentrated resources and garnered new ones to implement a districtwide literacy approach in K–3, including upgrading classrooms and libraries and leveraging a strong partnership with local philanthropy led by the William Penn Foundation.

By 2015, the district was seeing encouraging improvement. The number of students scoring below basic dropped by 20%, and the number of students scoring advanced proficient grew by the same amount.[4] In 2015, SDP had five schools rated at the highest performance level "model" based on reaching state proficiency standards and the district's performance scorecard; by 2018, there were 12. SDP also cut the number of schools in the "intervention" category by half (School District of Philadelphia, 2019).

Increased confidence in the district's strong financial stewardship and clear reform agenda resulted in an infusion of resources. The mayor and city council helped with a local cigarette tax, and both the city and state began contributing significantly more in 2016 (M. Stanski, former CFO of the SDP, personal communication, July 11, 2019). By 2018, the district no longer ran a deficit.

In a final inspiring example, when Baltimore City Schools (BCPSS) Superintendent Sonja Santelises faced a $130 million budget deficit in 2016, she sought philanthropic funding for an outside analysis of district spending and shared the results widely within the district and state. At the same time, BCPSS leaders engaged in a transparent process of reviewing and debating how the budget cuts would play out in schools if new dollars were not raised. Principals and community members were invited to look closely at school-level budgets to consider alternative approaches for creating a balanced budget. This generated widespread consensus that nonessential services had already been cut and that further reduction would do more harm to an already challenged district. In response, the legislature authorized a $160 million package over 3 years, until the new equity-based state funding system kicked in.

SUPPORTING DECLINING ENROLLMENT DISTRICTS
TO FIND THE SILVER LINING

There is no getting around the pain of losing jobs, shuffling schools, and disrupting long traditions when enrollment declines. Downsizing (or "rightsizing," as it sometimes is called euphemistically) is a multiyear effort that will involve the entire community—including unions, parents, city leaders, and the school board—in making choices and trade-offs. State governments also have a powerful role to play in supporting transition spending and in changing the policies and practices that get in the way of organizing resources more effectively. District leaders, communities, and unions need to work together to change contract provisions that may make sense in isolation but together make redesigning schools nearly impossible. Most states have an opportunity to revise funding formulas to ensure that students who live in poverty get the resources they need—by both "weighting" funding by need and ensuring that the formula works as intended. Philanthropists also can play a huge role by supporting the transition to new technology, innovative school designs, and capacity-building.

If done well, this entire process can bring the community together around what it values most. At best, it catalyzes new ways of "doing school" that improve results and the experiences for teachers and students.

NOTES

1. Education Resource Strategies (ERS) analysis of nationwide enrollment data (U.S. Department of Education, n.d.)

2. According to New York City Charter School Center (n.d.), charter enrollment grew by 95,000 from 1999 to 2016; an ERS analysis of New York City Department

of Education data shows an enrollment decrease of 91,000 (U.S. Department of Education, n.d.).

3. ERS analysis of nationwide enrollment data (U.S. Department of Education, n.d.).

4. Internal data shared with Aspen–ERS Chief Financial and Strategy Officer Network, Fall 2018.

REFERENCES

Bandiera, O., Prat, A., Sadun, R., & Wulf, J. M. (2014, April 30). *Span of control and span of attention.* Harvard Business School Strategy Unit Working Paper No. 12-053; Columbia Business School Research Paper No. 14-22.

Baskin, K. (2017, July 31). *Creating better bus routes with algorithms.* MIT Sloan School of Management. mitsloan.mit.edu/ideas-made-to-matter/creating-better -bus-routes-algorithms

Boston Public Schools. (2016). *Investing in student success: 10 big ideas to unlock resources in Boston public schools.* www.bostonpublicschools.org/cms/lib07 /MA01906464/Centricity/Domain/184/Investing%20in%20Student%20Success .pdf

Center on Reinventing Public Education. (2017, September). *Better together: Ensuring quality district schools in times of charter growth and declining enrollment.* www.crpe.org/publications/better-together-ensuring-quality-district-schools

Cleveland Metropolitan School District. (n.d.). *The Cleveland plan.* www.cleveland metroschools.org/Page/532

Education Resource Strategies. (n.d.). *Bold steps to better schools: Cleveland metropolitan school district.* www.erstrategies.org/stories/bold_steps_to_better _schools_cleveland_metropolitan_school_district

Education Resource Strategies. (2015, May). *Spending in Philadelphia schools: Summary of ERS analysis in the school district of Philadelphia.* www.erstrategies .org/tap/spending_in_philadelphia_schools

Education Resource Strategies & Oakland Achieves. (2017, June). *Informing equity: Student need, spending, and resource use in Oakland's public schools.* www .erstrategies.org/tap/informing_equity

FundEd: Charters. A national overview of charter school funding policies. (2020). *EdBuild.* charters.funded.edbuild.org/national#local-taxes_

Johnson, A. (2017, March 27). Hackathon's goal: Improve Boston school bus scheduling. *The Boston Globe.* www.bostonglobe.com/metro/2017/03/26/hackathon -aims-improve-boston-school-bus-times/cv2OZwG4rHarYvQoXGsbhO/story. html

Karnash, C., & Quinones, T. (2013, March 7). *School reform commission votes to save four schools, 23 to close.* CBS Philly. https://philadelphia.cbslocal.com/2013 /03/07/school-reform-commission-votes-to-save-four-schools/

Kelley, D. (2015, May 29). *School district says spending on students lowest since '08.* Metro. www.metro.us/philadelphia/school-district-says-spending-on-students -lowest-since-08/zsJoeC---BoUBRFuMOXASQ

McBride, L., Vaduganathan, N., Puckett, J., Rimmer, N., & Henry, T. (2013, January). *Adapting to enrollment declines in urban school systems.* Boston Consulting

Group. www.bcg.com/publications/2013/adapting-enrollment-urban-schools .aspx

Miles, K. H., & Frank, S. (2008). *The strategic school: Making the most of people, time, and money.* Corwin Press.

Miles, K. H., Pennington, K., & Bloom, D. (2015, February). *Do more, add more, earn more: Teacher salary redesign lessons from 10 first-mover districts.* Education Resource Strategies & Center for American Progress. www.erstrategies.org /cms/files/2450-do-more-add-more-earn-more.pdf

Neilson, G. L., & Wulf, J. (2012, April). How many direct reports? *Harvard Business Review, 90*(4). https://hbr.org/2012/04/how-many-direct-reports

New York City Charter School Center. (n.d.). *Charter school enrollment and trends.* www.nyccharterschools.org/charter-enrollment-trends

Owens, A., Reardon, S. F., & Jencks, C. (2016). Income segregation between schools and school districts. *American Education Research Journal, 53*(4). cepa.stanford .edu/wp16-04

Rich, M. (2012, July 23). *Enrollment off in big districts, forcing layoffs.* The New York Times. www.nytimes.com/2012/07/24/education/largest-school-districts -see-steady-drop-in-enrollment.html

School District of Philadelphia. (2013, April 26). *The school district of Philadelphia: FY 2014 proposed budget in brief.* www.philasd.org/budget/wp-content /uploads/sites/96/2017/09/fy14-proposed-budget-in-brief.pdf

School District of Philadelphia. (2019). *2019 action plan.* www.philasd.org/actionplan/

Travers, J., & Hitchcock, C. (2015, May). *Following the dollars to the classroom door: Why and how effective student based budgeting must be paired with strategic school design.* Education Resource Strategies. www.erstrategies.org/tap /following_the_dollars_to_the_classroom_door

Truong, D. (2018, October 20). When "the heartbeat" stops: Rural schools close as opportunity and residents flee. *The Washington Post.* www.washingtonpost.com /local/education/when-the-heartbeat-stops-rural-schools-close-as-opportunity -and-residents-flee/2018/10/20/bfc2d06a-b52f-11e8-a2c5-3187f427e253_story .html?utm_term=.6af2667bb02e

U.S. Census Bureau. (2019). *2017 public elementary–secondary education finance data.* www.census.gov/data/tables/2017/econ/school-finances/secondary -education-finance.html

U.S. Department of Education, National Center for Education Statistics. (n.d.). *ElSi database table generator.* nces.ed.gov/ccd/elsi/default.aspx?agree=0

U.S. Department of Education, National Center for Education Statistics. (2017, October). *Digest of education statistics, Table 236.70: Current expenditure per pupil in average daily attendance in public elementary and secondary schools, by state or jurisdiction: Selected years, 1969–70 through 2014–15.* nces.ed.gov /programs/digest/d17/tables/dt17_236.70.asp

U.S. Department of Education, National Center for Education Statistics. (2019, January). *Fast facts: Enrollment trends.* nces.ed.gov/fastfacts/display.asp?id=65

Warren, P. (2019, March 4). *Declining K–12 enrollment forces major budget cuts in many districts.* Public Policy Institute of California. www.ppic.org/blog /declining-k-12-enrollment-forces-major-budget-cuts-in-many-districts

CHAPTER 9

Cost-Effective Special Education
Good for the Budget, Great for Kids

Nathan Levenson

When I went off to college, my father gave me simple, time-tested advice. "Nate," he said, "You will meet lots of new people, and if you want to get along, just don't discuss politics, race, or religion." Decades later, when I headed off to my first day as a school district superintendent, Dad updated his advice and counseled, "Whatever you do, don't mess with special ed if you want to get along."

Fortunately for the kids in the district, I did not heed his advice, but Dad's caution says so much about the state of special education in America then and now. Even if some are unhappy with the current state of affairs, it strikes many as treacherous territory into which they will never dare enter. And yet, a great many challenges plague special education. Parents are often at odds with school and district leaders about what is fair and needed for their kids. And despite ever-increasing spending, students with disabilities tend to have unacceptably low levels of academic achievement and skills for life after graduation. The uptick in special education spending also can have adverse consequences for other key components of schooling, such as increasing class size, squeezing out arts programs, and hampering new efforts in STEM or behavioral supports.

Two things are true: Kids with disabilities deserve better; and more spending has not helped them in the past. Therefore, there is little reason to assume that even more dollars in the future will turn the tide.

Before we go too far down this road, however, let us put some important guardrails in place. More spending will not help, but that does not mean we should just cut or limit spending for special education. We owe kids with special needs a better life trajectory, and simply cutting back on staff or services will not make that happen. It will only make a bad situation worse.

So what *should* we do? Two changes could make a big difference for students, teachers, parents, and budgets. First is to get comfortable talking about special education spending. We should not vilify the budget staff who say costs are rising, should not disparage board members who lament that special ed spending is squeezing out other important needs, and should not malign any idea that saves money as per se bad for kids. We need to be able to talk about helping kids and the budget in the same conversation. Dads should not be afraid that their sons will try to improve special education. They should be disappointed if their sons do not.

The second change is to shift the conversation from costs and compliance to a focus on one overarching goal: increasing the effectiveness and cost-effectiveness of serving students with special needs. Fortunately for kids and taxpayers alike, my colleagues and I, working with pioneering districts across the country, have found a way to do both at the same time.

A FOCUS ON COST-EFFECTIVENESS

Shifting the debate from, "Are we spending too much or too little?" to, "Are we getting enough impact for the money spent?" is the key to helping kids with disabilities in an era of tight budgets. To do this, districts must:

1. Know what works for raising achievement
2. Know the actual cost of specific services and strategies
3. Shift resources to services and strategies that improve outcomes at reasonable cost
4. Rethink how special education is managed

In the paragraphs that follow I will discuss the teaching and learning strategies that actually help students with disabilities achieve at higher levels; the importance of knowing in greater detail what things cost, as it is hard to manage spending if the right data are not available; how funding what works will require adding more to some roles and services while trimming other spending, because helping kids with disabilities achieve at higher levels requires spending differently; and how to manage special education differently so as to turn into reality these ideas that are great for kids and good for the budget.

Know What Works for Raising Achievement[1]

Thanks to meticulous research by individuals like John Hattie and groups such as the What Works Clearinghouse and the National Reading Panel, a clear set of best practices for raising achievement have emerged (Levenson, in press). These focus on students with mild to moderate disabilities, who constitute roughly 80% of all kids with disabilities. These are the students with individualized education plans (IEPs) who can and should go to college and/or have rewarding careers. (Students with severe disabilities such as intellectual disability or profound autism need something different.) Best practices for the vast majority of students with disabilities include:

- Ensure that students receive 100% of core instruction in reading and math. If they do not receive all of the material or get a watered-down, below-grade-level curriculum, how can we expect them to master state standards or the skills needed for success after graduation?
- Focus on reading as the gateway to all other learning. If kids struggle to read and comprehend, then science, social studies, and even math become difficult to master.
- Provide extra instructional time to master grade-level content. Even with quality core instruction, students who struggle need even more instructional time than their nonstruggling peers. That typically amounts to 30 extra minutes a day at the elementary level and 60 at the secondary level. This time is needed to remediate skill gaps from prior years, reteach key concepts, and preteach upcoming material.
- Guarantee that core and intervention teachers have deep content knowledge. Nothing matters more than the teacher's skill and knowledge. Instructors trained in how to teach reading or with deep expertise in math are non-negotiables for student success.
- Address the social, emotional, and behavioral needs of students. The best academic practices cannot get traction if children are not ready to learn, able to focus, and engaged in their education.

The first step in knowing whether a district's approach to helping kids with special needs is cost-effective is to gauge whether the district is spending on these best practices. Unfortunately, some of the most common and costly efforts in use today are in direct conflict with what works. They include:

- Pulling students out of core instruction in reading and math to put them in special education services
- Devaluing the importance of reading on grade level by utilizing unskilled, untrained, noncertified paraprofessionals to support reading
- Over-relying on "push-in," the practice of giving extra help by sending a second adult into the classroom during core instruction and co-teaching, which does not provide a minute of extra instructional time
- Assigning special education teachers and paraprofessionals to academic support regardless of their training, skills, or aptitude in the subjects being taught

Historically, more districts have embraced these less-than-best practices than have shifted to what works. This preference for such practices stemmed from the false belief that more adults and smaller group sizes mattered more than time on learning and the skill of the teacher. Happily, the balance seems to be moving in the right direction.

One district I visited in Vermont, for example, exemplifies how far many schools have strayed. A well-run, high-spending district was committed to helping kids with disabilities. It embraced inclusion and cared deeply. It should be a great place to be a student with a mild to moderate disability. Nope! Students with IEPs were always included in the general education classroom, but paraprofessionals provided most of their reading instruction. Special educators who struggled in high school math tutored in math. The classroom teacher assumed that the special education staff would provide most of the instruction to catch these kids up, but they often were pulled out of core instruction for speech therapy and other services. In short, children who struggled got less core instruction than classmates who did not struggle. They received instruction from adults who were caring but who were not content-strong teachers (or teachers at all), and they never got extra time to learn. They got more adults, but not more quality.

Yet doing the right thing works only when it is done well. Poor implementation and inappropriate IEPs undermine these effective and cost-effective strategies. Measuring academic return on investment (AROI) closes the loop on doing what works and doing it well. AROI is the systematic, structured process of knowing what works, at what cost, for which kids. The idea is simple: Gather baseline data on student levels of content and skill mastery, identify or create a control group, measure growth, and see whether outcomes actually improve—and make sure to track the cost associated with serving each student. More on this point later.

The challenge is that few school systems gather such data. Too many rely primarily on professional judgment, observation, and faith in their practices. Kids with disabilities deserve better.

When districts *do* take the time and effort to measure what works, insights abound. One district, for example, was implementing a well-designed, best-practices reading program but was puzzled about why results did not improve after a few years of hard work and much professional development. On review, district leaders discovered that teachers and principals *thought* they were following the new plan to the letter, but actually many old habits had crept back in. Rather than trashing the program and buying a new one, district leaders recommitted to the existing one, but with more objective monitoring of fidelity. Within a year, reading levels climbed.

Another district happily discovered that a secondary math intervention program got excellent results—18 months of growth on average. A deeper dive into the AROI data revealed great success for kids who were 2–3 years behind, but not for kids with elementary-level skill gaps like fractions and number sense, or kids who failed math because they disliked school. No one best practice is best for every child who struggles. That district—smartly—kept its math intervention for some kids, instituted a different one for others, and switched from math help to counseling for a third group. As result, all three groups of students started making more than a year's growth and the achievement gap began to close.

Know the Actual Cost of Specific Services and Strategies

It is naive to think that districts can thoughtfully manage special education spending if they seldom talk about costs or rarely have the requisite cost data. In many districts, the shortest path to vilification is to talk about those costs rising. Sure, some board members may grumble about the share of the budget that goes to special ed or note that special ed staffing grows while other departments are cut, but any serious conversation about spending seems to quickly devolve into someone shouting, "You are trying to balance the budget on the backs of the neediest children!" One assistant superintendent I know left his district in part because of his discomfort with the superintendent's plan to measure special education costs per student and per service provided. He felt that was unethical, declaring, "We should spend whatever it takes."

Kids with disabilities do deserve more and better services, but doing so in a cost-effective manner is an act of kindness, not cruelty. Getting more comfortable talking about spending and shifting the conversation from total spending to cost per service helps expand services, not reduce them. That begins with knowing how much things actually cost.

One district, for example, discovered that two of its schools used different approaches for supporting students with disabilities who struggled to read. Each school had one full-time staff member dedicated to this effort. School A followed the National Reading Panel's recommendations, while school B embraced Reading Recovery. Both are best practices according to the What Works Clearinghouse, and AROI data showed that both achieved 1.5 years growth for the typical struggling student. Nice!

What was not so nice is that, as seen in Figure 9.1, Reading Recovery cost $5,000 per student, while the equally effective alternative cost $1,875. Fiscally, it seems wasteful to spend 2.5 times as much to get the same result, and morally it is not good either. When schools embrace high-cost strategies, they inadvertently ration these services. In school A, 40 kids got high-quality reading help—but in school B, just 15 did. Each school had one full-time equivalency (FTE) teacher, but one FTE teacher could serve a lot more students in school A. In school B, where there was not enough certified staff to help everyone who struggled to read, lots of struggling readers got push-in help from a less-skilled paraprofessional and fell further behind.

Knowing the cost per service provided to each student also helps build support for increased investment in highly skilled staff. Special education in America has a crush on paraprofessionals, despite mountains of research

Figure 9.1. Comparison of Two Equally Effective Reading Interventions

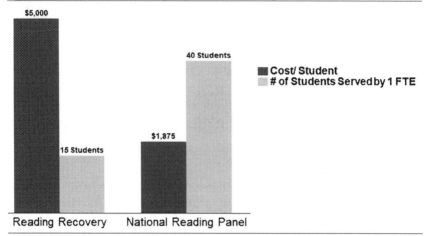

spanning decades that report no positive (and actually negative) academic gains for kids with mild to moderate disabilities.

The number of special education paraprofessionals increased by 22% (IDEA Section 618) over the past 10 years for which we have data, while student enrollment inched up just 2.6% (U.S. Department of Education, National Center for Education Statistics, 2017) during the same period. Yes, paraprofessionals are critical and valued for kids with severe disabilities and their health, safety, or behavior needs. But for kids who struggle to master grade-level content, paraprofessionals are asked to do much more. When my firm collected schedules from nearly 20,000 paraprofessionals from more than 125 districts across the country, we saw a great many paras spending most of their day providing academic support.

In one school, for example, 74% of all elementary para hours were dedicated to academic instruction, mostly in reading. When asked why they used paraprofessionals (which they had a lot of) and not certified reading teachers (which they had very few of), school leaders' answer was simple: They could not afford more certified staff.

A cost-per-student-served analysis was startling and revealing for school and district leaders. The process was straightforward. Step one is to determine the cost of each paraprofessional. Even this basic first step shocked the system. When leaders were asked, "What does a paraprofessional cost?" the quick answer was, "Not much, about $11,000." While $11,000 a year is not much, just about $12 an hour, it also was not true. Most paraprofessionals had health insurance, and some had seniority increases as well. While a handful of paras did earn about $15,000 a year, the full cost of most paras in the district was $39,000. Not such a low number, although definitely less than the cost of a certified teacher.

If we stopped the analysis at cost per adult, paras in fact are less expensive than teachers. But what happens when the conversation shifts to cost per service, per student served? Turns out each para helped about 10 students, for a cost of $3,900 per student. The district kept para-supported group sizes small, typically one or two kids at a time. District leaders hoped that intensity of support would offset the lower skill level of the instructor.

In the same district, a full-time reading teacher or special educator with strong reading expertise earned about $85,000, including benefits, but that person helped 35 students. Groups of four to five kids, all with similar academic needs, were no problem for these teachers. Which means the highly skilled teachers cost less than $2,500 per student served—a better bargain and much better for kids. This type of cost-per-student-served analysis was brought to K–12 schools by Marguerite Roza, a fellow contributor to this book.

Armed with this understanding, the district swapped one-third of its paras for certified staff, which expanded the number of students served by skilled teachers, and reading proficiency increased by 5 points. It also freed up funds to hire a couple of mental health counselors. This was the result of a financial analysis driven by wanting to help, not harm, kids with disabilities.

Getting comfortable collecting cost data and discussing relative costs of various strategies should be encouraged. Legally and morally, kids with disabilities should not be denied services based on the cost, but that need not mean costs are not tracked or discussed. Often a win-win is possible—an intervention strategy that is both great for kids and good for the budget.

Shift Resources to Services and Strategies That Improve Outcomes at Reasonable Cost

Ultimately, the only way to ensure that all students are prepared for success after graduation in a world of high standards and tight budgets is to shift spending away from practices not proven to be effective or not implemented in a cost-effective manner. The key word here is "shift," not "add." This means that as districts do more with best practices for raising achievement, they will have to add staff in some areas, but they will be able to trim in others, as less effective practices are replaced by more impactful ones.

Making special education more cost-effective for students has to also make the lives of special educators better. This means increased spending to support teachers is needed. But offsets are possible so that the extra help that both kids and staff need can be cost-neutral.

The spending implications of using cost-effective best practices are sweeping. Districts that have embraced these practices and seen achievement rise use their precious dollars very differently than the typical district. The major increases in spending include:

- More instructional coaches. If general education core instruction is foundational (and it is), then investing in instructional coaches is key to building the capacity of classroom teachers to better serve students with special needs.
- More teachers with expertise in teaching elementary reading. Given the centrality of reading as the gateway skill, gap-closing schools invest heavily in highly skilled teachers of reading. These can be general education staff, certified reading teachers, or special educators with deep expertise in reading. Their title or certification is not the important qualification; their skill and training are.
- More teachers with expertise in teaching secondary reading. The need to read and comprehend well does not end with 4th grade. Unfortunately, too many middle and high school kids still struggle to read. Schools owe them a skilled reading teacher, too.
- More general education math and English teachers. Providing extra time to master the three Rs closes the achievement gap only when the extra time is spent in direct instruction from content-strong teachers. All those intervention classes need great English and math teachers in the front of the room.
- More behavior specialists and mental health counselors. Even the best academic strategies will not get traction if schools fail to meet the social, emotional, and behavioral needs of students. And if problematic student behavior overwhelms classroom teachers, they will resist their greater role in serving all students.

Such a long list of added staff might surprise readers expecting a call for less spending in special education. I hope it comforts those focused on improving and expanding services. Fortunately, both taxpayers and students can benefit from cost-effective strategies. While some areas need more spending and staff, these additions can be offset by:

- Slightly larger groups of students (with like needs). Nothing controls the cost of serving students with disabilities more than managing average group size. The math is straightforward. A teacher running five groups a day of three students each costs twice as much per student as the same teacher serving six students at a time. As a corollary, twice as many teachers are needed to serve the same group of students if the group size is three, not six. If six kids seems too large, how about a group size of five? Perhaps surprisingly, these larger groups can be better for kids and teachers. That can happen in a number of ways, starting with forming groups of kids with similar needs. Contrast the typical reading group of three students, one struggling in phonics, another in decoding, the third in fluency, versus a group of five students all struggling with phonics. The homogeneous group of five is easier to teach, and the impact will be greater. And when the group of five is taught by a highly skilled reading teacher, rather than three kids with a paraprofessional, the impact is multiplied yet again.

- Fewer paraprofessionals for academic support. As certified staff provide more instruction, the role of paras is redefined to focus on health, safety, behavior, and students with severe needs.
- Fewer generalist special educators. As extra-time classes and reading interventions become the norm, fewer periods of generalized homework help, like those in resource rooms, are needed, reducing staff needed to cover these classes.
- Fewer meetings, less paperwork. U.S. public schools employ more than 300,000 special educators, and more than half of their time goes to meetings and paperwork. (That is based on my firm's study of more than 7,000 special education teacher schedules from more than 100 districts.) Nationally, this equates to an annual investment of more than $12 billion in meetings. Locally, streamlining meetings and paperwork by 20% adds the equivalent of four FTE teachers to a district of 5,000 pupils. Do not worry that this is not possible, that compliance will drop or overtime work will be required. The science of process mapping can almost always free up far more time in nearly all districts and still maintain 100% compliance. Staff morale usually rises, too, because special education teachers get to do more of what they love, which is to help students. Final proof point: In every district I have studied, some staff have already figured out how to reduce meetings and paperwork by 30% or more compared with others in the district. The path to more time with kids already exists.

On the whole, best practices cost no more, and in some cases cost less, than traditional practices. But they help kids a whole lot more.

A few cautionary notes. Shifting resources is hard and can be anxiety-producing. It is important that the new and better services are added before, or concurrent with, reducing current services. Fears that cuts are definite, while additions are just a promise, rightly worry many. Remember, kids with disabilities deserve better, not less.

Yet no one needs to lose their job to fund these shifts. Given how difficult the job is, many staff leave their district or the profession every year. All the shifts can be paced to match attrition.

One district that dramatically closed its achievement gap between general and special education employed all of these shifts in funding. While achievement skyrocketed, spending declined slightly and services expanded greatly. For example, they swapped 10 paraprofessionals for three reading teachers. When three special educators left the district, they were replaced by one math teacher, one English teacher, and one behavior specialist. Paired with a slight increase in group size and a reduction in meetings and paperwork, the remaining special educators did not have an increased workload or workday. By increasing honors and AP classes by one student on average, the high school freed up funds for a full-time reading teacher, too.

Over time, this district of roughly 5,000 students shifted a whole lot of funds and staffed seven reading teachers, three instructional coaches, two secondary reading teachers, one behavior specialist, two extra math teachers, and four additional English teachers. While it did end up with fewer paraprofessionals and special educators, it still had over 60 paraprofessionals and more than 40 special educators. There is no reason to fear, as many do, that such shifts eliminate all paras or decimate the ranks of special educators. Shifts will always play a critical role in any best-practice plan. Small shifts through attrition can make a big impact for kids and the budget, without negatively impacting hard-working adults.

Rethink How Special Education Is Managed

Perhaps the most overlooked aspect of cost-effectively serving students with disabilities is the modified role of leaders and managers. Cost-effectiveness does not just happen. It is managed day in and day out. To successfully implement the first three steps, districts must rethink how special education is managed and who is part of the leadership team. Too often, managing special education is siloed and distributed in ways that are not good for kids, adults, or the budget.

It's siloed because the special education director is typically in charge of almost everything, including academics, finance, staffing, and of course compliance. For example, in the vast majority of districts I have worked with, the chief business officer *receives* the special education budget rather than partners with the special education director to develop it.

The academic segregation of responsibilities is on full display where there are disappointing achievement results. In a common annual ritual, superintendents present state test score results to their school boards. When the PowerPoint advances to the slide showing a huge special education achievement gap in math, all eyes in the room turn to the special education director, who makes some promises about how next year will be better. No one asks the chief academic officer, the K–12 math director, or the principal as instructional leader to remedy this wrong. It is all on the special education director and the designated special educators.

The overly distributed management style becomes clear in just a short conversation with special education staff. Ask a special educator, "Who is your boss?" and an eye roll or pause is the most common answer. "I report to the building principal," they might respond, but then add quickly, "But if

I have a special education question or problem, I call central office and see who I can get to give me an answer." Ask principals and they are likely to say that realistically special educators do not report to them because they do not know enough about special education to be effective managers. Ask paraprofessionals whom they report to and the most common response is a nervous laugh, a look away, and a quiet, "No one, really." The special education staff in most districts gets less help, direction, feedback, and guidance than any other role.

One thing nearly all can agree on is that typically the central office assigns special educators and related services therapists to specific schools, but day-to-day schedules are developed entirely by the individual teacher or therapist. Let me say again: In a district where elementary teachers are scheduled down to such details as "teach reading from 9:00 to 10:30" and "make sure 20 minutes is for phonics and 30 minutes for whole-class instruction," and where high school teachers are told how many periods to teach, when to teach, and who will be in each section, special education staff are just directed to a specific school and asked to make it all work out and schedule all services to keep in compliance.

To close the achievement gap, increase equity of access and outcomes, and do so cost-effectively, districts need to manage special education differently. The new best practices cannot be effectively implemented via the old organizational structure, or with a hands-off, walled-off approach to leadership. Two changes to how special education is managed will smooth the path toward more effective and cost-effective services: (1) helping proactively to manage staff time, and (2) integrating special ed leadership.

Help Manage Staff Time Proactively

Whoever is managing special educators and related specialists should rethink what is included in the role. The staff deserve more support and guidance than they receive in many districts. This is a contributing factor to the high burnout of special educators.

The overwhelming majority of special education spending and services provided is connected to staffing. Staff, kids, and the budget all benefit when there is more direction and planning for how staff use their precious time. Most often, special educators are handed a caseload and asked to make it all work. Rather than leaving it to each person to balance IEP meetings, evaluate IEP eligibility, provide services to students, and handle myriad other tasks—and hoping it all fits within the day—districts should set guidelines for how best to use the time available. Frontline staff should, of course, be part of the conversation. In the many dozens of focus groups I have led, special educators feel that their time is not optimized and that they are stretched thin.

What do these guidelines look like? They answer questions such as:

- How many hours a day should a special educator work directly with students?
- How many hours a week should a school psychologist provide counseling?
- Should students getting reading services in a "small group," as stated in the IEP, have group sizes of two, four, or six?

In nearly 200 school districts I have studied, fewer than a handful of leaders have answered such questions for the staff they manage. Why is this a big deal? Because without a collective answer, every staff member is left to figure it out for themselves, and this is not cost-effective or good for kids. It is also stressful for staff.

On average, as seen in Figure 9.2, a special educator spends about 48% of the day with students, or around 16 hours a week. But in some schools, even within the same district, some special educators spend 65% of their time with students. That equates to one extra day of teaching each week, the same as adding almost 50% more teaching staff! Managers can assist more teachers to do likewise by streamlining meetings and paperwork.

School psychologists are also in great demand as the need for social–emotional counseling has been on the rise. So what priorities are set for

Figure 9.2. Special Education Teacher Time With Students

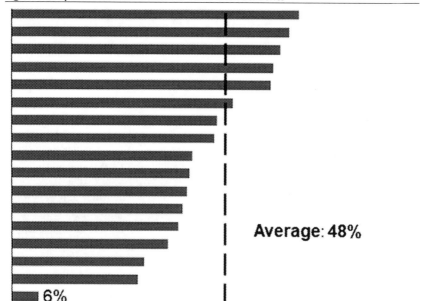

Average: 48%

6%

these very talented professionals? The most common guidance from their supervisor, typically a central office administrator, is to make sure the district is in compliance with IEP evaluations, do what the building principal asks, and provide as much counseling as they can. Priorities may not be stated this explicitly or glibly, but that is the message sent, and it plays out in a lot of odd ways. In some schools, principals ask school psychologists to sit in on all the Response to Intervention meetings, while others do not. In some districts, an initial evaluation takes about 20 hours from start to finish, while in a neighboring town, it takes only 10. The result of not having clear expectations on how best to use their time means that one school psychologist might do the equivalent of a single initial IEP evaluation a week and get pulled into many meetings and thus have just 3 hours available for counseling (after allowing for lunch and prep time). The other psychologist would do the same number of evaluations and have 18 hours available for counseling. It is easy to guess which school will ask for another psychologist in the next budget. With guidance, direction, and support from their managers, school psychologists can do more of what they love, what they are trained to do, and what kids need!

Lastly, the question of group size is just too important to be left to each staff member. Classroom teachers do not get to decide whether their 1st-grade class has 20 or 25 kids in it, and high school math teachers do not get to decide whether Algebra 2 will have 15 or 30 students. Leaders and managers make this call. Most IEPs state whether support is one-on-one or in a small group, but the definition of "small group" is left to each teacher. Some special educators schedule small groups with as many as six students in elementary grades, others three, and some just one student at a time. There is no single right group size, but not having an answer is not right either. First-graders might have smaller groups than 5th-graders. Kids with severe needs should have smaller groups. Social skills groups might be bigger than reading groups.

My research indicates that staff preferences, rather than student needs, drive group-size decisions in most schools. Some teachers always have very small groups, year after year, while others have larger ones. This is true even when they change grades or receive students served by other teachers who had very different group sizes.

Small groups are a big deal. Shifting from an average group size of two to three may not seem earth-shattering, but it means a single teacher could help 50% more kids each week.

If groups are formed with students with similar needs, great things can happen. Imagine one group with three students, one with a math goal, another with an executive functioning goal, the last with reading difficulties. Compare that with a group of five students who are all struggling in phonics. The larger group is easier to teach and more impactful. It also costs $2,500 less per student served.

It is very hard to implement thoughtful guidelines for the use of staff time if scheduling is not treated as strategically important. The schedule is where guidelines become reality, or do not. It is just too important to delegate scheduling to every individual special educator. Managing the special education budget well includes managing staff schedules well—because staff time is where most of the money goes.

There is no reason to assume that every special educator is a great scheduler. It is not taught to them, nor is it screened for during interviews. Building schedules in partnership with a manager and with the help of an expert scheduler is the last ingredient in managing special education cost-effectively.

Integrate Special Education Leadership

I can think of no job more stressful, overwhelming, and lonely than leading a special education department. A director might have 40 to 60 direct reports; most unhappy parents eventually land in their office; the state department of education monitors compliance like a hawk; the staff is burning out; and during budget season, lots of people blame the director for cuts elsewhere in the district. By the way, the students also are struggling academically, socially, emotionally, and behaviorally. Everyone wants the director to fix this, but few see it as their job to help in that effort. It is a no-win situation.

Just as academic best practices call for an important role for general education, it follows that general education leadership will be critical to increase the cost-effectiveness of serving students with disabilities. Rather than expecting a special education leader to carve out a unique slice of teaching and learning, the head of teaching and learning must have the primary responsibility for ensuring that all kids, including those with mild to moderate disabilities, learn to read, excel at math, and master grade-level content. Chief academic officers, assistant superintendents for teaching and learning, and such are the experts in academics and accordingly should drive this important work. Special education leaders are the copilots.

In elementary schools, general education leaders, namely, principals, assistant principals, and reading coaches, also must lead the effort to ensure that all kids can read and comprehend what they read. Separate is never equal, but often it seems that elementary schools have forgotten this lesson. One school I visited exemplifies too many others. It had an experienced, skillful instructional leader as principal. She was a former reading teacher, and she knew that reading was job one. She observed classroom instruction every day, gave pointed and thoughtful feedback to classroom teachers on how to improve their craft and better serve struggling readers, and made sure that no one skimped on the 90-minute daily reading block or cut short the daily phonics instruction. When it was time to hire staff, she put would-be teachers through mock lessons and quizzed them on the recommendations of the National Reading Panel. She was so committed to a hyperfocus on reading that she used nearly every minute of building-based professional development to hone teachers' skills in that vital subject. For added measure, the top-notch reading coach she hired spent hours each day supporting these efforts.

Sounds like a great plan, and it was for some—but not for kids with special needs or their teachers. This very skilled principal never observed or gave feedback to special education teachers. They reported to the special education director downtown, who, of course, had staff in many schools and seldom visited unless there was a crisis or an irate parent. When hiring special educators, which the principal did participate in, she quizzed them on their understanding of the law, not on how to teach reading. On professional development days, the special educators went to the central office to learn the latest state requirements, and they missed the sessions on how to better teach reading. And no, the reading coach didn't work with special educators because "there was no time in the day." No surprise that general education achievement climbed while that of students with disabilities stagnated. Districts make big investments in their special education staff, but they often do not invest enough in helping them be the best at their craft.

Other departments also need to integrate more closely with special education. This includes measurement, accountability, and the business office. If we want special education to focus on what works, it seems reasonable that folks trained in collecting and analyzing data and program effectiveness do this for all programs, including those that serve students with special needs. In the same spirit, the business office should be an active partner that adds value in predicting special ed staffing (as it does for general ed) and helping track and manage spending. This might seem like common sense, but it is not currently common practice. Making special education more cost-effective is no easy task, and it requires a team effort. Formally tasking these departments with helping to manage special education is key to managing it well.

SHIFTING PRACTICES FOR A NEW ERA

The world has changed. The kids coming to school today have more needs, but schools have fewer resources. A focus on improving the effectiveness and cost-effectiveness of special education is the only path forward that does not lead to worse outcomes, fewer services, and more teacher turnover.

Fortunately, this journey can be good for kids, staff, and taxpayers, all at the same time. Perhaps the roughest patch will be to embrace new approaches, get comfortable talking about costs, and focus on what works. But that is not a trip special educators have to take alone. General education leadership, general education teachers, and other managers will lighten the burden and make this a team effort.

NOTE

1. For more details on where and how to shift services, see Levenson (2020).

REFERENCES

Levenson, N. (2020). *Six shifts to improve special education and other interventions*. Harvard Education Press.

U.S. Department of Education, National Center for Education Statistics. (2017, October). *Digest of education statistics*. nces.ed.gov/pubs2018/2018070.pdf

Conclusion

Frederick M. Hess

One of the more frustrating education debates of the past quarter-century has been the debate about whether money matters. Indeed, back in 1996, this question served as the title of Gary Burtless's volume, *Does Money Matter?* What a peculiar question. After all, it's tough to think of anywhere else in American life where we'd have that discussion. If we're talking about buying a house, choosing a cell phone plan, or paying for preschool, folks on the Left and the Right sensibly assume that more money makes it easier to afford better options. Of course, money matters.

This is why it's been so strange to see the school-spending debate dominated by this straw man of an argument. The fact is, when I talk to school-spending skeptics, they don't argue that money *can't* help—their concern is primarily that more funds will be spent in ways that won't make a difference for students. Meanwhile, I've found that most who champion more spending will concede readily (if quietly) that *of course* it matters how those funds are spent. As Adam Tyner, director of research at the Thomas B. Fordham Institute, points out, while we've been arguing about straw men, it turns out that just about everyone agrees that the answer to the question, "Does money matter?" is, "Yes . . . BUT." What matters is not only *how much* money is spent, but *how* those dollars actually are spent.

And yet, as Brandon Wright, co-editor of this volume and editorial director of the Thomas B. Fordham Institute, observed in the Introduction, politically expedient hyperbole too often has drowned out more useful discussion of how to make sure that funds are spent wisely and well. That is a luxury we can no longer afford, in an era of stretched budgets and expanding demands on schools. However much we should be spending on schools, our students will be better served if each of those dollars is spent thoughtfully.

What makes the preceding contributions so timely and relevant is that, whatever readers' various views on how much we should spend or how those funds should be allocated, they offer a stimulating, concrete, and practical path to spending school funds in ways that are most likely to make a difference for students.

FOUR TAKEAWAYS

While we've spent the past quarter-century debating whether money matters, some things that should've been obvious got overlooked. That much is made clear as one peruses the takeaways that dot the preceding chapters. Here, it's worth taking a moment to flag four of those that we find most relevant for thinking about how we move forward.

1. There May Be Headwinds Ahead for Increased School Spending

Schools should spend money effectively. That's what we call a no-brainer, and it's true all the time. But it's going to be increasingly important given the headwinds school spending is likely to face in the years ahead. After all, as Matthew Ladner, senior research strategist at the Arizona Chamber of Commerce, observes, "Our public schools enjoyed decades of nearly uninterrupted funding increases—typically gauged in inflation-adjusted, per-pupil dollars—throughout the 20th century and into the 21st. . . . Circumstances, however, may be conspiring to bring a profound change to this trend." In particular, Ladner suggests that a graying population is likely to strain budgets, especially as Washington struggles to pay for sprawling entitlement programs. In an aging nation, with massive demands on the health care and retirement systems, there are likely to be growing headwinds for school spending.

2. Document Dumps Don't Equal Transparency

There's widespread agreement on the theoretical value of "transparency" when it comes to school spending, but it's also the case that transparency can obscure more than it reveals. For starters, policymakers and school system leaders already tend to imagine that they are transparent. They suffer from the convenient conviction that dumping 400-page budgets and piles of hard-to-decipher numbers online equates to transparency. Marguerite Roza, director of the Edunomics Lab at Georgetown University, notes that "Education leaders nationwide now have access to a treasure trove of per-pupil, school-specific spending data for every school in the country" (Ch. 5, p. 69). What's needed is a focus on how to make this information available, concrete, and useful for all stakeholders.

3. Tight Budgets Can Be a Boon

While it may be unserious to suggest that "money doesn't matter," there is a wrinkle: On occasion, more money actually can be counterproductive, by serving as an enabler. Organizations that enjoy steady streams of revenue can find it tough to make unpleasant decisions, such as shuttering ineffective programs or terminating ineffectual employees. There's a natural human instinct to avoid such decisions, when possible, which is why tight budgets sometimes can be a useful spur or provide the political cover that allows a leader or a board to blame "necessary circumstances" for hard choices.

4. They May Not Look It, but Spending Decisions *Are* Bold Reforms

Some who call for "bold" reform may be tempted to dismiss attention to spending and budgeting as inadequate. That's a mistake, because a focus on spending is deceptively bold—it involves altering priorities and what schools actually do. After all, for all the ambitious talk about policies and goals, budgets are what determine what actually happens in schools and classrooms. They may seem "incremental," but they drive important decisions about staffing and programs. Moreover, while bold policy reforms serve as magnets of controversy, budget decisions tend to stick.

TEN PRACTICAL RECOMMENDATIONS

We embarked upon this volume with the aim of setting aside familiar debates over how much schools *should* spend and instead focusing on practical recommendations as to how schools and systems might better spend the funds they have. We think the contributors have succeeded admirably in that task. With that in mind, it's worth flagging a few of the main suggestions they have provided.

1. When Investing in New Tech, Remember to Ask "Why?"

American schools have a long-running, unrequited love affair with education technology. From ballpoint pens to blackboards, and from radios to desktop computers to iPads, outlandish claims have been made that this next advance is going to change everything. Time after time, we've been disappointed. Scott Milam, Carrie Stewart, and Katie Morrison-Reed of Afton Partners observe that technology can make a big difference for learners, but that what really matters is how it's used. As they put it, "The smart incorporation of technology indeed will allow for increased 'bang for the educational buck.' But when incorporated poorly, technology can distract, detract, and waste a lot of money." They note that the districts that have the best experiences with technology start by asking, "What are the goals and objectives for technology-enabled classrooms?" and by thinking clearly about how success will be measured. The most important question should never be, "How much technology does a school or system have?"; it should be, "What's being done with it?"

2. Curb the Accumulation of New Pension Debts

By shifting from traditional pension plans to those that more closely link benefits to contributions, states can start to address massive pension shortfalls, freeing up enormous sums for salary and operating expenses. Chad Aldeman, senior associate partner at Bellwether Education Partners, notes that, "Teachers may not know it, but their paychecks are being reduced due to rapidly rising benefit costs." While spending on salaries and wages rose just 21% over the past 2 decades, spending on employee benefits increased by 98%. Failing to tackle pensions means that many schools will wind up devoting a staggering share of revenue to fund retirees. Tackling pension reform, on the other hand, offers an opportunity to start bending the curve and to redirect dollars into schools and teacher salaries.

3. Remove Policy Barriers That Impede Smarter Staffing Models

State laws and directives are littered with rules, regulations, and routines that make it challenging for schools and districts to rethink staffing. Bryan and Emily Hassel, co-presidents of Public Impact, point to line-item budgets that limit reallocation of funds, to rigid class-size limits that make it difficult for teams of teachers and paraprofessionals to collectively serve a group of students, and to certification requirements that inhibit cross-functional teams or efforts to develop new approaches to mentoring and induction. As the Hassels explain, too many existing policies serve to "lock in one-teacher, one-classroom structures. In such cases, policymakers could clear the way for schools to make the shift." That holds the promise of opening up staffing approaches that are more cost-effective *and* more instructionally effective.

4. Tight Budgets Offer Opportunities for Improvement

While nobody likes tight budgets, they can have a silver lining. Karen Hawley Miles, president and CEO of Education Resource Strategies, explains, "Budget pressure always generates a call to reduce district office spending because it doesn't immediately impact the classroom. This often leads to such stopgap measures as freezing hiring, drawing down reserves, or deferring maintenance." Such measures are a short-term patch, Hawley Miles argues. District leaders instead should respond to tight budgets, she writes, by focusing on a more "sustainable strategy" and seizing the chance to "reenvision the district office role and focus district-level spending on a few powerful improvement strategies." She suggests that districts start by addressing three questions:

- "Where can the district find efficiencies?"
- "Are there opportunities to lower costs . . . without compromising quality?"
- "What resources and decisions might district leaders devolve from central to school level to foster stewardship and better match spending to school-specific needs?"

5. Cost-Consciousness Is an Important Part of Improving Special Education

If American education has a third rail, it's probably special education. Between student rights safeguarded by federal special education law and inevitable concerns about shortchanging students with special needs, there's often a reluctance to talk about cost-effectiveness when it comes to special education. That's a big problem. Nathan Levenson, managing director of the District Management Group, writes, "It's naive to think that districts can thoughtfully manage special education spending if they seldom talk about costs." He observes, "The number of special education paraprofessionals increased by 22% over the past 10 years" or nearly ten times the rate at which student enrollment grew. And yet, Levenson writes, "In many districts, the shortest path to vilification is to talk about those costs rising. . . . Any serious conversation about spending seems to quickly devolve into someone shouting, 'You are trying to balance the budget on the backs of the neediest children!'" Levenson argues that children with special needs deserve better services, and this means that thinking about cost is an essential and ultimately an *ethical* act.

6. Leaders Need to Sweat the Small Stuff

From No Child Left Behind to the Common Core, from "personalization" to teacher evaluation reform, education tends to be dominated by a fascination with big ideas and "ambitious" reforms. That impulse can get in the way when it comes to getting more bang for the buck. Mike McShane, director of national research at EdChoice, wryly observes that "it's no fun to track the price differential between timber and prefabricated concrete blocks, but deciding between them can have a huge impact on a school's financial prospects." Indeed, suggests McShane, "[it's the] prosaic details [that] make the difference. It simply won't be enough to operate a better-than-average school. Competition for teaching talent will increase, and schools will need to figure out how to offer more attractive salary and benefit packages. Families will expect more, and more diverse, offerings, from extracurriculars to robotics."

7. Approach Spending Decisions as an "Either–Or" Choice

Decisionmaking always involves trade-offs. Marguerite Roza suggests that a useful tool for doing this is a "would you rather" approach, which helps focus on what is at stake. She explains, "Used as an ongoing part of routine budget and finance deliberations and functions, 'would you rather' thinking lets leaders pause to examine what services have been built (or are proposed), at what cost, for what value, and to whom." For example, she notes, district policymakers wrestling with teacher benefits might ask teachers whether they would rather have "$14,000 to apply to benefits of [their] choosing, with any savings added to [their] salary" or $14,000 in "district-chosen benefits." Roza has found that giving stakeholders an appreciation of trade-offs helps them think more honestly and creatively about what they really value. And honest, creative thinking is exactly the kind of thinking that schools need if they're to get more bang for the buck.

8. Focus on Outcomes That Matter Most

Any attempt to talk about "bang for the buck" requires that we actually know what we mean by "bang." That means we have to talk about outcomes. Which outcomes are the right ones to focus on? What metrics should be used to calculate "return on investment"? There is a tendency—when these weighty questions arise—to simply default to reading and math scores on state assessments. And that threatens to import some of the bad habits that have been evident in school accountability. Wielded carelessly, convenient metrics may unintentionally serve to narrow instruction, miss much that parents think important, or push teachers to emphasize test preparation and small-minded routines. Measures are selected with an eye to what is important, and not what is easy to measure.

9. Reexamine the Role of Research

Education research today tends to reward using cool tools to study big data sets in order to offer simple answers to complex questions. The problem is that it does little to help schools find ways to get more bang for the buck. Figuring out exactly where dollars are going is more of an accounting exercise than a question of conventional research. The information can be messy, and tracking dollars to particular people or programs—or linking those to results—can be onerous. All this time-consuming, ambiguous work can be unappealing to researchers who are rewarded for published analyses that offer clear findings. After all, if the impact of money depends on *how* it's spent as much as *how much* is spent, then the impact of spending is going to vary in complex ways from one school—or school system—to the next. Ensuring that education research is useful, wary of blind spots, and reflective about what it can and can't say begins with rewarding researchers for asking the right questions—even when the answers may be murky, contingent, or ultimately unsatisfying.

10. Technology Is Mostly About *Enabling Teachers*, Not Replacing Them

The productivity gains attributed to technology in other sectors are real. But technology has to be used as a tool to amplify and support talent—not imagined as some kind of replacement for it. Enthusiasm for wildly new, "disruptive innovation" sometimes has blinded us to the fact that, 90% of the time, technology's biggest impact is on optimizing or enhancing familiar tasks and routines. This frees up time, talent, and dollars for better uses, fueling improvement. If teachers are able to spend less time entering data or collecting papers, they can spend more time teaching, mentoring, or preparing lesson plans. What Bryan and Emily Hassel have sketched is a model that asks how schools and systems can most effectively use the talent they have on payroll. The key to all of this is to focus on the problem to be solved and not simply on adding devices or imagining that technology somehow can replace the innately human, complex work that good educators do.

CLOSING THOUGHTS

This volume really should be read as an invitation to practitioners, parents, and policymakers to rethink school spending, rather than as the definitive word on the right recipes for change. The approaches and analyses offered here are intended to encourage all parties to bring their experiences and best thinking to bear as schools seek ways to ensure that each dollar actually is making a difference for students.

In the end, none of this is really about money—at least, it's not about money the way we frequently talk about it in popular culture or in heated debates about taxes and government spending. None of the contributors here are urging anyone to slash school spending or to boost it. None of them are seeking to dictate how school funds should be spent. None are advocating that education funds be used to plug holes in state and local budgets. Rather, this is all really about how schools spend the funds we have—no matter how much or how little—in a way that makes the biggest difference for kids. No matter how boring talk of declining enrollment, staffing models, and construction costs might seem, that's something that ought to resonate with all of us.

Especially at a time when huge obligations to teacher pensions and health care, the demands of a graying population, and a global pandemic create a challenging fiscal environment for schooling, demonstrating that education funds are being spent wisely and well also may matter greatly for efforts to build support for new school spending. Indeed, Mike McShane has a telling tale to share regarding Alberto Carvalho's two successful bond elections in a decade as superintendent of Miami-Dade. As McShane has put it in the past, Carvalho told him, "I was able to go to voters and make the case that 'the last time you gave us money, we spent it well.'" Doing that not only ensured that the funds actually worked for kids, but also helped build support for spending. As Joanne Weiss, a former high-ranking Obama official, put it, "People are not averse to paying more taxes, they just want to know that there's value attached to it." Perhaps not surprisingly, when the public thinks money is well spent, it's more likely to provide more of it.

When it comes to school spending, getting more bang for the buck is never just a matter of spending on "what works." It's a complicated calculus of student needs, available resources, political realities, and local context. That's why decisions on school spending are never cut-and-dried but are best seen as an opportunity to discover more promising paths forward. Our hope is that this volume may help practitioners, parents, and policymakers journey a few steps along that trail.

About the Contributors

Frederick M. Hess is director of education policy studies at the American Enterprise Institute, where he works on K–12 and higher education issues. He is the author of the popular *Education Week* blog "Rick Hess Straight Up," is a contributor at *Forbes* and *The Hill*, and has served as an executive editor of *Education Next* since 2001. He has published in scholarly outlets such as *American Politics Quarterly*, *Harvard Education Review*, *Social Science Quarterly*, *Teachers College Record*, and *Urban Affairs Review*, and in more popular outlets such as the *New York Times*, *USA Today*, the *Wall Street Journal*, and the *Washington Post*. His books include *Letters to a Young Education Reformer*, *The Cage-Busting Teacher*, *Breakthrough Leadership in the Digital Age*, *Cage-Busting Leadership*, and more. He also has edited influential volumes on the Common Core, entrepreneurship in education, education philanthropy, the impact of education research, and the Every Student Succeeds Act. Before joining AEI, he was a high school social studies teacher. He also has taught at the University of Virginia, the University of Pennsylvania, Georgetown, Rice, Johns Hopkins, and Harvard University.

Brandon L. Wright is editorial director of the Thomas B. Fordham Institute. He is the coauthor of two books: *Failing Our Brightest Kids: The Global Challenge of Educating High-Ability Students* and *Charter Schools at the Crossroads: Predicaments, Paradoxes, Possibilities*. His writing has appeared in outlets including the *Wall Street Journal*, *Washington Post*, *New York Daily News*, *National Review*, *Newsweek*, *Education Week*, *Phi Delta Kappan*, *School Administrator*, and dozens of state newspapers. He holds a JD from American University Washington College of Law and a BA from the University of Michigan. He is also the author or coauthor of several research reports, and appears frequently on radio stations across the country.

Chad Aldeman is a senior associate partner at Bellwether Education Partners, where he serves as editor of TeacherPensions.org. Previously, Chad was a policy advisor in the Office of Planning, Evaluation, and Policy Development at the U.S. Department of Education, where he worked on Elementary and Secondary Education Act waivers, teacher preparation, and the Teacher Incentive Fund. He has published reports on, among other things, teacher pensions and teacher salary schedules. His work has been featured in outlets like the *Washington Post*, *New York Times*, *Wall Street Journal*, *InsideHigherEd*, and *Newsday*.

Bryan Hassel is co-president of Public Impact. Dr. Hassel's work includes co-leading Public Impact's efforts to help schools create an Opportunity Culture by extending the reach of excellent teachers to more students, for higher pay, within budget. He also consults widely with states, districts, nonprofits, and foundations on an array of education issues, including school finance, educator talent, charter schools, and school turnarounds. Bryan is the author of the book *The Charter School Challenge: Avoiding the Pitfalls, Fulfilling the Promise*, and is the coauthor of many others. His work has appeared in publications such as *Education Next* and *Education Week*.

Emily Ayscue Hassel is co-president of Public Impact. Emily was previously a human resources consultant and manager for the Hay Group. She leads design and strategy for the Opportunity Culture initiative, a national effort to redesign schools to extend the reach of excellent teachers to more students, for higher pay, within budget. Emily also led prior research on education talent, funding allocation, best practices in talent management, district school turnarounds, and growth of the highest-performing charter schools for disadvantaged students. Her work has appeared in *Education Week*, *Education Next*, and other publications.

Matthew Ladner is a senior research strategist at the Arizona Chamber of Commerce and Industry and executive editor of the weblog *redefinED*, which is hosted by Step Up for Students. Previously Ladner served as a senior research fellow at the Charles Koch Institute, senior advisor for research and policy at Excel in Ed, and vice president of research at the Goldwater Institute. He has provided invited testimony to Congress, state legislatures, and the U.S. Commission on Civil Rights. Ladner has written numerous studies on school choice, charter schools, and special education reform.

Nathan Levenson is managing director of the District Management Group, where he works closely with superintendents and their leadership teams to help raise student achievement and improve the work life of teachers despite tight budgets. He was previously the superintendent of Arlington Public Schools in Arlington, Massachusetts. He is the author of, among other things, *Smarter Budgets, Smarter Schools: How to Survive and Thrive in Tight Times* and *A Better Way to Budget: Building Support for Bold, Student-Centered Change in Public Schools*.

Michael Q. McShane is director of national research at EdChoice. A former high school teacher, he earned a PhD in education policy from the University of Arkansas. He has written broadly about the challenges of educational improvement and looked closely at intriguing models for rethinking educational delivery. McShane has authored or edited books including *New and Better Schools*, *Education and Opportunity*, *Teacher Quality 2.0*, *Common Core Meets Education Reform*, *Educational Entrepreneurship Today*, and *Bush–Obama School Reform: Lessons Learned*. His analysis and commentary have appeared in outlets such as the *Wall Street Journal*, *USA Today*, the *Washington Post*, *National Affairs*, *Forbes*, *Education Week*, and *Phi Delta Kappan*.

Scott Milam is a cofounder and managing director of Afton Partners with Carrie Stewart. He leads initiatives to support public K–12 school districts, charter networks, and their stakeholders in navigating complex financial issues, including working closely with philanthropic investors, grant programs, and school leaders to develop and implement sustainable financial plans for innovative schools and school models.

Karen Hawley Miles is chief executive officer and president of Education Resource Strategies. She has worked with school systems nationwide to analyze and improve their funding systems, school-level resource use, and human capital and professional development systems. She has authored numerous articles and co-authored *The Strategic School: Making the Most of People, Time, and Money*. Karen serves as a senior advisor to the Aspen Institute Education and Society program and has taught and trained school leaders at Harvard University, in school districts, and for New Leaders for New Schools.

Katie Morrison-Reed is a senior director at Afton Partners, working at the intersection of finance, strategy, and operations. Throughout her time at Afton and in previous positions, Katie has focused on the role finance plays in promoting and sustaining innovation in education systems. Katie supports education leaders across the country in developing financially sustainable schools and systems with an eye toward equity.

Marguerite Roza is a research professor at Georgetown University and director of the Edunomics Lab, a research center focused on exploring and modeling education finance policy and practice. Dr. Roza leads the McCourt School of Public Policy's Certificate in Education Finance program, which equips participants with practical skills in strategic fiscal management, policy analysis, and leadership. Her work has been published by the Brookings Institution and in *Public Budgeting and Finance*, *Education Next*, and the *Peabody Journal of Education*. She is author of the highly regarded education finance book, *Educational Economics: Where Do School Funds Go?* Dr. Roza was a senior economic advisor to the Bill & Melinda Gates

Foundation. She also served as a lieutenant in the U.S. Navy, teaching thermodynamics at the Naval Nuclear Power School. She earned a PhD in education from the University of Washington and a BS from Duke University, and studied at the London School of Economics and the University of Amsterdam.

Carrie Stewart is a cofounder and managing director of Afton Partners with Scott Milam. Carrie advises state agencies, school systems, and philanthropies on education finance matters. Under Carrie and Scott's leadership, Afton has advised on over 120 initiatives throughout the country, with specific emphasis on funding equity, fiscal transparency, and resource allocation strategies.

Adam Tyner is associate director of research at the Thomas B. Fordham Institute. Adam brings not only expertise in education policy but also experience from his previous work at Hanover Research, where he consulted with district administrators from some of the nation's largest school systems on questions of school funding and how to improve academic outcomes. In his current role, he develops, manages, and executes education research projects on a variety of topics.

Index